STALKED IN THE WOODS

True Stories

~~~

Steph Young

TABLE OF CONTENTS

Introduction

The following true stories, set within the Woods and areas of the most remote wilderness, encompass a terrifying array of baffling, frightening, and unexplained disappearances, deaths, and very strange encounters.

In the Woods, things are never quite what they seem....

Chapter 1: The Vanishings

Richard Hasbell was described by his friends and family as a quiet and shy man who, because of his mental disability, liked to take off on his own for long bike rides and hikes. It was said to have been his way of coping with his illness. Although he suffered with this illness, his brother and other members of his family said that he was always good at reporting back to them, and he had always been able to look after himself, and had never come to any harm. His brother did add however, that he had not gone quite so far into the wilderness on his own before.

It was July 10th, in 2005, when he arrived at Denali National Park, in Alaska. When he registered at the Park and applied for his camping permit, he said he would be returning by the 18th. He took the shuttle bus provided at the park to Wonder Lake. He never returned. A search began for him including both ground and air search efforts, in a landscape of rugged wilderness. Two days into the search, a pilot saw his tent near the peak at an elevation of just over

4,000 feet, five miles North-east of the Lake. The pilot had been out looking for a plane that had crashed.

The following day Park Rangers flew to the spot where his tent had been seen. It was confirmed to have been his, along with the bear-resistant food canister. There was no sign that the camp had been disturbed by bears or any other predators. There was still food inside the bear-proof container, some of which had been eaten but a plentiful amount remained. His tent also appeared not to have been tampered with or suffering from any damage. They knew this was the missing man's provisions because they also found a journal, with his hand-writing. The last entry in the journal had been on the 17th. Strangely however, all three pairs of his shoes were gone, as confirmed by his brother. His brother also said he was physically fit enough, as he was an avid walker who would take weights in his backpack to improve his stamina and endurance.

Searchers checked all drainages, and any possible routes that he could have taken from the tent. They found footprints indicating that the area had been trodden by other hikers, but according to searchers, none of these matched up with the missing man. The area was thoroughly searched for days and yet no traces of him could be found by the seventh day. They found a disposable camera, a sock, and other footprints, but said that these were not connected to the missing man. He has never been found....

~ ~ ~

Richard Lyman Griffs was an inventor. He was also a well-travelled man. This time, he had ventured to the wilds of Alaska with the specific intention of testing his latest invention. It was fall of 2006, and he had invented a Survival Pod for camping. The problem was, he hadn't told anyone where he was going or what he was intending to do, and so he wasn't reported missing for months.

When a search was started, Nabesna District went out to look for him after Mounties had worked out that he had bought a bus ticket heading North. The bus ticket would have taken him to the Alaska Highway, and they discovered that he had left some personal items at a lodge near White River. He had apparently told some guests there that he was heading up-river to test his survival Cocoon-Pod. It was bright orange. Neither he nor the bright orange Cocoon-Pod have ever been found.

Alaska Dispatch News followed up on his disappearance retrospectively, speaking with former Mountie Sgt. Ben Sewell; "Nothing has ever surfaced," he said, although he wonders if one day, at least a piece of the orange Cocoon might show up, somewhere.

Alaska Dispatch said the disappearance never made it into the Newspapers at the time, years ago, and adds, "His vanishing is like all the others, who over the years have turned to ghosts;" their disappearances leaving no trace of them at all behind...

~ ~ ~

At a home in Lakewood, in the Green Mountain area of Colorado, a party was in full swing. Conversation however had turned to the controversial topic of police shootings, and the host, paramedic Eric Pracht, felt the best thing to do would be to step outside for a few moments to cool down and get some fresh air. The 25 year old left the party with his fiancée without taking anything with him apart from some trash to take out, and stepped outside for a few moments. He never came back inside. It was July 22, 2016 and he didn't have any shoes on, so he surely couldn't have gone very far? He said he was just taking a short stroll. His car was still outside, and he didn't have his car keys anyway.

Lakeland Police Spokesman Steve Davis said; "He never had any talk of suicide or thoughts like that. It's almost as if he just walked away." But he had no money with him, no belongings...The search for him turned into a week long search; with everyone completely baffled as to how he could have been outside the apartment one minute, barefoot, and gone the next. Police say he had an argument with one of the guests and left for a walk. When he took the trash outside with his fiancée, he told her he needed to take a short walk to get some air, according to the police, because he'd got worked up about the possibility that he could be a target like the police had become, for wearing a uniform. His fiancée went back inside. He didn't come back.

During the week-long search, the police brought in cadaver dogs to see if they could pick up his scent and discover where he may have gone; but they couldn't find his scent and nothing else turned up. "We exhausted all leads," said Davis. There had been no activity on the missing paramedic's cell phone, his debit cards, or on internet social media such as facebook.

His family said he loved his job and he had never walked away from anything before and it wasn't in his character to do so. They said he was very responsible, dedicated to his job, and would never not turn up for work. Strangely however, 17 hours after he disappeared, some sources said his cell phone gave off a signal. The signal pinged off a cell tower at the base of green mountain. His sister, Erica, said the cell tower recorded the moment his *phone* turned on, and this was several hours after he had left the party, but no calls were made from it and no texts sent. That was the last time his phone was used. That information did help the authorities to hone in on the area of Green Mountain where the phone had been however.

His apartment is a short walk from the base of Green Mountain and National Forest, with an entrance close-by. Perhaps he wandered into the Forest, had an accident, got lost; but then, he would have been only a short distance from home, and surely, even if he had a minor accident, he could have made it out of the forest and alerted someone? Or, surely he would have been found in the resulting search which lasted a week and covered all of that area both inside and outside the forest.

A month later and his family and friends were still searching for him; searching through the roughest terrain they could find, just in case he was in a gully off Green mountain. They hacked through all the bushes in a desperate attempt to find any kind of clue inside the Forest.

As September came, his friends and family were still arranging search parties; not one of them able to understand how he could simply have vanished just like that inside the Park. He is still missing.....

~ ~ ~

In September 2015, 36 year old Timothy Nolan was found dead in Yosemite National Park, following an extensive search effort. His last contact with his family had been on the 1st September, after which he planned to set off on his solo hiking trip in Yosemite. He didn't return from his 5 day trip and his family alerted the authorities. Parks Spokesman Scot Gediman described the search for him, utilizing S&R teams and dogs, as well as aerial searches. Posters with his details had also been distributed and displayed. Mariposa gazette described the search as "extensive" ever since he had been reported missing.

The Sierra Sun Times said it was actually park visitors who later came across his body. Strangely, his body was later found on "a well-travelled trail in the High Sierra Cap Loop," in the back-country. This was after the same area had been previously searched. Investigators, after the discovery of his body, were "working to determine a cause of death," according to the Parks Spokesman, implying that it wasn't immediately obvious how or why he had died. According to local news journal *The Fresno Bee*, this was the third man to be found dead in the National Park that month...

~ ~ ~

28-year-old Christopher Sylvia had set out on a lone hike over several days, along the Pacific Crest Trail in Southern California, in February 2015. The day after he set out, he phoned his room-mate to ask him to come and collect him the following day at a Buddhist temple in San Diego County. His room-mate agreed he would meet him there, but when he arrived there the next day, and waited, Christopher never showed up.

Newspaper reports state that his friend believed he must have continued hiking after changing his mind about being picked up, and perhaps his cell phone was out of range and he couldn't call his friend to let him know. However, when he failed to make it to his final destination either, and his friend still couldn't get hold of him on the phone, that's when concern for him set in.

A search was initiated, and quite quickly some of his hiking gear was located along the trail, not far from the agreed pick-up point at the temple; however, despite a continued and extensive search, there were no signs of the man himself. Some hikers also found his sleeping bag and his backpack. Thirteen miles off the highway, his I.D. was found.

He was described as an experienced hiker, and Newspaper reports described his hiking trail as a well-travelled and well-populated route, safe for solo hikers. It was not described as completely remote nor a very difficult or risky hike, and although it was rugged in parts, it was not heavily forested. Despite an extensive search for him however, no trace of him was found. Sheriff Search and Rescue efforts were called off after an extended search for him had taken place over a number of days, which turned into two weeks. A spokesman for the San Diego County Sheriff's department told reporters, "It's now been two weeks since he was heard from and we are still running any leads."

His mother, Mrs Nancy Sylvia, said her son had gone on the hike not long after breaking up with his girlfriend and wanting to clear his head," but she didn't say he was in any way suicidal, and besides which, if he had been, where was his body? "He was sad, but when I spoke to him he sounded good," she added. "I don't understand why he just left his gear behind."

A hiker, Mary Litch, who had come across abandoned shoes, which at the time she thought could have been his, said that she is a regular hiker along the trail. "I consider it a very safe place," she said, "Many people hike here alone. I've come across Mountain Lions but they're always shy. I'd have more concern about people than them."

The lengthy search had got progressively harder due to the change in weather, with fog and rain, but over

30 volunteers had kept hard at it in the search for him. People on the Pacific Crest Trail mailing list received the following email; It is with deep regret that I inform the hiking community; the search has been terminated....One recent theory is that a camp of drug smugglers might have been encountered, leading to his disappearance and demise. There are other possible theories being under consideration by LE.' The writer did not however state what those other theories might have been, and the mystery still remains as to what could have happened to the missing man.....

~ ~ ~

In September 2015, officials from Skamania County called off their search for a man who had last been seen over a month earlier. County Sheriff Spokesman Dave Brown said that their search for Austin Oldfield had proved fruitless. Two hunters had seen him last, and they said that he had told them he was lost. They offered to show him the way, but they say that as they were doing so, he took off running in the opposite direction. At that time, he had no shoes on.

The hunters found this very bizarre.

The missing man had been on a planned lone two-week trip, sending a text to his girlfriend on September 17th of 2015, this being his last known communication. Coming from Kentucky, he had set out for Gifford Pinchot National Forest to go camping and hiking. Two days later he was reported missing, after he failed to phone his relatives as he had said he would. His car was located at the camp-site, and the two hunters had seen him close to Lone Butte, approximately one mile from his camp-site. When searchers began to look for him, they found his camp-site, but no sign of him. At this point there were over 50 people searching for him, along with K9's. Some searchers rappelled down the crevices.

As the days passed, more people joined in the search and his sister and her husband came to look for him. According to his sister, he had carefully planned the trip, months in advance. She said that he had been in good spirits prior to his trip, had been visiting friends along the way before he entered the National Park, and had been looking forward to the trip for months.

She feels that far from any suicidal inclinations, he had been taking the trip for a sense of renewal and fresh starts, after having quit smoking and drinking some months before this and was now drinking health drinks instead. He also had a daughter, which his family say he would have never left behind forever, and would have stayed in contact with her throughout the trip. Despite the busy period in which he went into the National Forest, with lots of hunters and hikers and campers; no-one else came forward to say they had seen him. His sister thinks that is the strangest thing about it....

~ ~ ~

According to the Prescott Courier of Arizona, in 1988 on the night of Halloween a man called Larry Rivers was driving along a dirt road in the desert when he came across a man walking. Slowing the car down and opening his window, he asked the man; "What are you doing out here?"

"I'm looking for the beast," the man on foot replied. The man's name was David Stone, and he was wearing just a T-shirt and shorts, despite it being almost winter. This was believed to be the last time he was seen alive. Nearly a week later, he was officially reported missing. His remains were not found until four years later when three hunters stumbled across them. The former Deputy Sheriff, William Cavliere said, "It's just about the strangest thing that ever happened round here."

When the man was reported missing, the search for him was massive. Planes flew over-head, teams of searchers covered and re-covered the ground with bloodhounds. There was no sign of him. His tracks were found; but it seemed they just stopped. The missing man, David Stone, had been travelling en-route from San Diego to El Paso in Texas, where he was to be best-man at a friend's wedding. When he didn't arrive for the wedding, his father contacted all of the Sheriffs offices between San Diego and El Paso. None of them had received any reports about the missing man, but the local Sheriffs did subsequently discover his car on route 80 in New Mexico, parked at an odd angle, nearly fifteen miles south of Forks Road.

The search for him lasted almost two weeks until it was called off. His remains were found when hunters, four years later, saw bones in a granite outcrop, about a mile from the highway. One of the hunters, Ken Melhberg, said he thought at first they were animal bones, but as he got up close to them, the first thing he picked up looked to him like a human jaw-bone. He knew then that the bones were not animal at all; they looked distinctly human. Although the hunter said the skull appeared shattered from the back, the exact cause of the missing man's death was unable to be determined by the medical examiner. Dr Mani Ehteshami said; "There is no reason to believe there was any trauma. He did not sustain any injury before or at the time of his death." Although his skull was in pieces, the Dr. believed this was due to animal predation.

Any personal items; such as his car keys, his wallet, and a necklace that he wore, and all of his clothing were all missing from the spot in which his remains had been found. The only thing that was found, were the remains of his shoes. Leader of the County Search team, Ralph Dawdy, said that their search for the missing man was; "one of the strangest" in his long years of search experience. When Stone walked into the Desert, he left behind him some very mysterious and hard to fathom 'clues.' He left his car near pyramid shaped mountains, and as searchers followed his initial trail leading northwest from his car, they came across a pile of small rocks that had been formed into a pyramid and enclosed in a triangle of rocks.

The following day, the searchers found another pyramid of rocks further on, and beside this was the missing man's rolex watch. Stone had been a very successful Stock-broker and wealthy enough to have afforded a rolex. A couple of miles further, they discovered written in the sand of the desert, the Fibonacci sequence; but instead of the traditional ending of the number 21, it ended at 18. Some say this was Stone's way of signaling he needed help. But, if so, why did he need help? What was happening to him?

The bloodhounds led the searchers on a 13 mile trek,

following his scent to close to Highway 80, where it stopped. In his abandoned car, they discovered a note which said; "They think the WORD is in the safe. Six knives in Rob's room. You buys your tea and yous takes yous chances Halloween...."

No-one has been able to work out what that meesage meant, nor what happened to him that night....

~ ~ ~

Talented musician and songwriter Jim Sullivan's début album was lauded by many as an incredible, evocative and haunting body of music. Entitled 'U.F.O.,' it was recorded in 1969, in Los Angeles. Despite the success of it among aficionados of that type of music however, he didn't hit the big time. His album had been recorded with session musicians who had backed stars such as the Beach Boys, but sadly for him, his profile failed to reach the heights of this band, and feeling frustrated by this, he decided to try his luck in Nashville and see if he could get his big break there. So, in 1975, he left his wife and young child, promising them that if he could get work as a musician in Nashville, he would stay there and send for them. However, he never made it to 'Music City' Nashville. He never arrived there.

While driving through the desert of the Southwest, he simply vanished without trace. His disappearance is as mysterious as the lyrics in his songs and his disappearance has never been solved or explained. Cryptically, the lyrics to his songs include such lines as: "I found a magic man. I bought a pound of magic and a kinda dream and plan," "Lotta tricks were pulled in a book I read. Only man I know that got pulled up and from the dead," and, "Looking at the sun dancing through the sky. Did he come by U.F.O.?"

Eerily, his lyrics seem to have been a possible foreshadowing of what was to happen to him. Everyone knows of the Roswell incident, but perhaps something just as mysterious and inexplicable happened in the same New Mexico desert twenty years later; or perhaps there is a far more mundane explanation. When Jim Sullivan left home and set out in his car along the New Mexico Desert highways, no-one could have expected it would be the last time he was seen. At sometime in the early hours of March 5th, 1975, he checked into a motel in the small town of Santa Rosa, two hours outside of Albuquerque on Route 66, after leaving his family home the day before. Perhaps he was very tired as he drove, because a Highway Patrol officer saw his car weaving along unsteadily, and instructed him to do a sobriety test.

He passed the test however, and as he was found not to be intoxicated, he was allowed to go on his way but was probably advised to stop for the night, because he then soon after checked into the motel. The next day, his motel room was found locked from the inside, the key left there and his bed looking like it had not been slept in. He was no-where around and his car was gone. Later, it was found about 25 miles away from the motel, parked up very close to a ranch property. The car was locked. It was parked in the middle of the road.

As told on Aquarium Drunkard's music blog, in 2010 Matt Sullivan, who shares the same surname but is no relation, became someone who found themselves intrigued by the tale, and he set out to try to investigate what could have happened to him. Sullivan, who runs an independent record label lightintheattic.net was a big fan of the vanished man's music. "The strings, the voice; it's dark and eerie. With or without his disappearance there's something in those lyrics that is incredibly eerie and mysterious."

Armed with film-makers, he set out to record his investigation. The family who lived on the ranch outside of which the missing man's car was found, had long since moved away, but he managed to track down the original news reporter who had covered the discovery of the car and the absence of Sullivan, and he also spoke to many of the missing man's friends. One music friend told Matt that he and the missing man had once sat together long into the night, talking about how they would disappear if they ever got to that point in their lives. The missing man said his way of doing it would be to walk off into the desert. Perhaps that is what happened then; but for the vast majority of those who knew him, they all said he

STALKED IN THE WOODS

would never have just walked off, and he would never have left behind his beloved guitar.

The one thing that everyone who knew the missing man emphasised, was that his guitar was found in his car; and they believed he would never have voluntarily walked off without it, even if he had somehow reached a point of despair; they just couldn't see that happening. If he had planned his disappearance too, they said he would in no way have vanished purposely without taking his guitar. He needed it to make any kind of living, even if it was just busking in the street for a few dollars a day. The wife he left behind too is not convinced he planned to disappear. She said: "He felt he could make better progress with his career in Nashville. Our plan was he'd go there. If he made it, even a little money, then we'd go there and join him. He was going to call en-route, from the next stop but then I never heard from him again. We found out he had never left Santa Rosa."

Matt Sullivan told New Mexico radio show *All Things Considered*, "He leaves LA with $120, starts driving, and 15 hours later checks into a motel in Santa Rosa. His car is found 25 miles away from the motel and he's never seen or heard from again." The ranch, outside which his vehicle was found parked in the middle of the road, was owned by an Italian family, and after a full-scale search was initiated by the local police, rumors started that the Italians living there were connected to crime families in the Mafia. The police believe that the missing man either knocked on the ranchers' front door, or, that the rancher's wife went out to the car accompanied by two farm hands, to find out why he had stopped his car so close to their property. Of course, the possibility then is that some kind of altercation took place in which some kind of foul play was at hand. This is all just speculation however because no evidence was found by the police to support this, and search parties found no trace of evidence indicating foul play had taken place. That of course leaves three other possibilities; one being that he had planned his disappearance before even leaving his family home, and had put his vanishing plans into place, among which would have to have included arranging for someone to come and pick him up. He could have been picked up that night out in the desert and disappeared to start a new life; and yet there wasn't a single person who knew him who could ever have imagined him abandoning music and never playing again. It was everything to him, and it was all he did. Even if he hadn't hit the big time, like plenty of others, they couldn't see him forever abandoning his one passion in life, nor could they imagine him never getting back in touch with the wife and son, Chris, he left behind. He has never contacted them, nor any of his hundreds of friends. No-one has ever been able to work out why he drove out along that road and parked outside the ranch either.

In his search for answers, Sullivan made calls, corresponded with people by email, went to the extent of hiring private detectives, and even consulted with palm readers and psychics, trying to find any clue that would lead them to finding out what had happened in the desert that night. Had he walked into the desert and died; wandered off into the barren uninhabited land to kill himself? And yet how far could he have walked away from his car that night? If he had walked away to die out there, searchers would have come across his body in the following days and weeks that they searched for him. Perhaps it's relevant that the ranch family moved quite soon after he disappeared, and the Sheriff who had been in charge retired. Then again, they are most likely completely unrelated.

On the other hand, with the album he had recorded being entitled 'UFO,' and his lyrics speaking of begin taken up into the sky, perhaps there is far more to this disappearance than we could imagine. He had written in his songs; "Looking at the sun dancing through the sky...did he come by UFO? I found a magic man. I bought a pound of magic and a kinda dream and a plan...." Of course, there is no evidence at all that it happened that way; no accounts or trace evidence to go on, but it also seems we will never know what really happened out there in the desert that night.

Al Dobbs was his close friend and the music producer who first discovered his talent, and he too was captivated by his songs. "His music was totally different. I had not heard anyone put words together like he did." According to Dobbs, at some time after checking into the motel, his good friend had got back on the road and "drove 26 miles down a dirt path going into an absolute wilderness." Dobbs speculates; "Did something go wrong, possibly, and you have a cover-up?"- alluding perhaps to an encounter with the ranching family, or others, out on that remote road; but he adds too, "Both he and his wife had a very long history of interest in U.F.O.'s. They were, as many of us were, fascinated by something from another world. We wanted to believe. I want to believe. I'd love to see them."

For at least 18 months, Sullivan's family, State police, and volunteers all combed the area in which his car was found, but they found nothing that could explain what had happened to him....

Chapter 2: Encounters Unknown

In rural parts of Northern England and up into Scotland, the Bogart should never be named; for if it was, none would be able to reason with it and it would become uncontrollable, and vicious. It would reap a path of destruction. If it came in your house, it would pull on your nose or ears. Often, horse-shoes could be found on the front door of homes, in the belief that this would shield their occupants from the invasion of a Bogart. The Bogart's own domain lay on the Moors, under bridges or in crags or caves. There are alleged disappearances of people associated with the Bogart, in earlier centuries.

Paul wrote to me about a number of very strange incidents that happened to him in "Bogart" country. "The first occasion was when I went to a place called Odgden reservoir in Bradford with a friend. We went up there in the evening around 5 p.m. It was still summer so it didn't get dark till around 11 p.m. We had the usual BBQ campfire etc... we didn't drink anything this particular night. There were animals, owls etc. Come around 10.30 p.m. it was getting slightly dark when we noticed a shift in the atmosphere around us, like we were being watched from all angles by something predatory. The trees and the wind etc... all stopped dead. And the animals went quiet. Nothing physically changed around us. I noticed a large type figure very briefly in the corner of my eye to my left which moved very fast within what I would estimate to be a good 30/50 yards in a split second. I thought my eyes where playing tricks on me. Then my friend said there is something over to the left looking at us from the brush. We had an awful feeling that we needed to get out of the woods and I noticed my big wood chopping machete was missing.

I could not see anything looking at us in the woods but could feel the atmosphere that we needed to leave. My friend almost ran for his life but I grabbed his coat and told him we do not split-up under any circumstance. We picked up big logs of wood and stood back to back, and I said, "It's time to get out of here - now." We wanted to pack our things up but the fire had died down. We put the coal and the wood and plastic etc onto our fire, which had embers and was very hot but no matter what, we couldn't get that fire to light.

We managed to get our things together and as we were leaving in the dark, we heard something very large and fast sort of run and leap into the area which the fire was. We tried to get out of the reservoir but it seemed almost like we were walking and not going nowhere for like 45 minutes; when it's maximum a 15 minute walk. My friend was seeing things on the path that he described as basically black puddles floating under his feet, that he kept freaking out and jumping over. We finally got out and felt much relief when we did, but when we were half-way down the big road with fields etc either side, we noticed what looked like a sheep, but for some strange reason it started beaming a light like a candle-sized light, and it seamed to be growing and pulsing. And it grew at least 8 feet wide. That's the first time and incident; I know it's long but I couldn't think of a shorter way to put it.

A second time up there, we had a camp-fire which was actually in the more dense woods, when to the left direction my friend said he saw something, and I saw a glimpse of something but couldn't see what he saw exactly. Anyway, we had a campfire and a few beers this time, and this time there was 3 of us camping this night. I forgot to mention; my friend had his dog with him, the same friend from the first incident. Anyway, we ate the food and went to bed and 3 of us and the dog shared the tent. We heard a few foxes coming to check the food wrappers and stuff, and the odd owl. Our other friend fell asleep, and almost as soon as he did, the dog started growling and shaking and was scared. He never did this with the foxes. We heard a heavy footed biped, not a fox, wandering around in the dark and we knew it was not a person and then just like that it was gone...

The 3rd incident was with me and 3 others, all different from the initial 2 friends. I went to Ogden to camp with one friend and this friend was skeptical about the two previous incidents we'd told him about;

he was mocking us a little; he's into bushcraft and he said he has camped many times and has never seen or heard anything, so he came with two other friends of mine and we had a fire and drinks, and all was good, the conversation flowing etc. The others both left around midnight but they ended up getting lost so we went to go find and guide them out of the woods. Then we went back to the camp. It was probably around 1 a.m. by this time. We had hammocks this time, not tents, and we were in our hammocks and must have been talking a good hour about random topics and I could hear a fox, which kept rushing past. It must have happened about 7 times at least.

There were several sounds which could have been rabbits or rats, voles or mice...but around 2/2:30 ish roughly I noticed a shift in the atmosphere. I never said anything to my friend and we kept talking away, then I could hear again large biped feet, that were really heavy but really fleet-footed too, which sounded like it was far in the distance yet close at the same time which was weird, but it seemed to me as though whatever this was, it covered a good 300 yard in less or around ten seconds. There is no way to me any man could do that in broad daylight never mind pitch-black in dense woodland. This was all coming from behind me. I turned around and had a look around, but there was nothing there. I could hear whatever it was move, from my left to the right about twenty yards in the wood, but couldn't see anything.

My friend was just talking away and I said nothing to him; I don't know why I didn't but I never spoke a word to him. I turned back around towards my friend when all of a sudden I heard the footsteps very large come right up to my hammock and tarp, and it literally felt like its face was almost touching mine, but everything on earth and if you believe in God also was telling me "DO NOT TURN AROUND" so I never did turn around. It moved off after a good two minutes of me crap...g myself and heart-racing, and it was wandering around again, twenty feet behind me. I then turned around again and it flipped from my side in a split-second and started doing the same, twenty feet behind me, at my friend's side this time.

After about five minutes after that, it just disappeared, and it was like the Woods returned to normal, and the animals came out again. I managed to get to sleep; never mentioned it to my friend. In the morning when light came and we both woke, we had a chat, and I asked my friend; "Did you hear anything last night?"

He said; "No, what do you mean?" I told him what I had heard, and he said, "No, never heard that, but why do you think I kept talking all night - Because I felt like there was a presence that really didn't want us in the woods at all....."

We packed up and left, and now to this day, my friend will never go back there when I mention it to him. He refuses to go in not so many kind words, and he had camped up there hundreds of times by himself, but never that area."

My personal opinion, after doing more homework on this and other things is that I think it's a possibility there's some kind of nature spirit at Ogden. All over is stories of the 'Bogarts' and all over is little green troll decorations in the trees that people have put up. They're put up because there is a tradition that some creatures called the Bogarts live up there and I believe this could be fairies or some kind of nature spirit. Its always happened on a place called 'Spice Cake Hills.'

Where we go, its near water and is woodland area although I don't think anyone out of the ordinary situation has gone missing. I would never go up there alone after dark; and I'm not the scared type. I will walk any area of Bradford at 3a.m. and not worry at all. You go to Heaten Woods and you never get a weird feeling once; Heaten Woods is ancient woodland, but Ogden has something a little bit more aggressive about it....

Another strange incident occurred in the Woods in northern England, according to a lady called Catherine, who wrote to me. "I just heard you on 'Where Did The Road Go?' podcast and your mention of the harlequin reminded me of a research area of my own."- I had mentioned in passing on a podcast, when asked about the recent phenomenon of clown sightings, that someone I correspond with had told me he has been haunted not by a clown but by a Harlequin figure at night, ever since a young boy. He also said that he believed and had been researching how clown sightings could tie in with the phenomenon of missing people.

Catherine continued; "I'm very interested in Germanic history and folklore, and there's a connection between the Wild Hunt and harlequins. I'm adding some photos I took from a book that has the most in-depth study on the subject 'The One-Eyed God: Odin and the Indo-Germanic Männerbünde' by Kris Kershaw. Given the connections between the Wild Hunt and people being taken, harlequins and disappearances would make a certain sense."

This was new to me, I had never heard of the Wild Hunt, (and am now doing in-depth research into this, which will be presented in the next book.) Catherine also said; "The podcast also reminded me of an experience I had with some genius loci, when I still lived in England. We'd been camping near the Ridgeway in Shropshire (near Much Wenlock). A friend and I had decided to go exploring the woods on the Ridgeway at night and ended up getting chased out by these huge beings that looked like they were made out of shadow. They were really tall, slender, and had roots for feet. They basically followed us back to the campsite and only stopped at the boundary there.

We also built up the fire like crazy because it felt somehow important to do so, but even though, it still felt as though they were pacing the boundary trying to get in. The old folklore about escaping things from the wild by coming back to cultivated land held true for us that night. I hope these pages from the book are helpful for your research (and are maybe helpful for that guy that kept seeing it). Best regards, Catherine."

I had to find out more, and Catherine was kind enough to expand upon her experience that night. I wanted to know; we're they dark shapes, black, solid, or semi-solid? How were they moving? How did she know what they were? I had heard about and written of 'black stick men,' 'shadow men' and other such sightings, but never of something that appeared to have roots for feet and that detail for some reason, I find particularly chilling.

Catherine was kind enough to draw what they looked like for me, and to try to describe them, I would say they are very large up-right figures, whose shape can perhaps best be described as like of a woman in an old-fashioned style of dress; a long dress that has a wide large skirt that expands from the waist down, and wearing some kind of cap. Of course, that at first glance is how to describe them but they are Not 'women in dresses' and from the end of the 'dress,' where the feet would be, are a series of long tree roots, and the dress appears as though made from the bark of a tree.

"They appeared solid, solid black. There was no transparency to them. Their movement was weird because it was almost like they didn't so much move as....'shifted'. Like they were just in one place, and then moved a bit further forward but you didn't quite see the movement. I don't recall the roots moving like feet at all. They were pretty fast though, and before I actually saw them, I heard kind of like footsteps on the path behind us as we were exiting the woods. There'd been this sense of 'you shouldn't be here' in the woods and like something was getting closer - zeroing in on us. So we'd left and heard the footsteps. At one point though, I turned around and saw these two genius loci, blinked a few times, and watched them cross a little stream no problem. I'd thought things like that couldn't cross running water, but that didn't seem the case. At that point, we ran. When I saw them, I really couldn't believe what I was seeing. I knew they were genius loci - or at least I called them that - because they felt very much connected to the place. They didn't seem happy that we were there at all and there was a sense of intelligence about them...."

I would love to know more about these entities, and if anyone else has had such an odd experience, like Catherine?

~ ~ ~

The experience a gentleman called Clint had, is just

as strange. Clint had also contacted me to relate a series of very unnerving incidents. "I was born in Granite City, Illinois, across the river from St. Louis MO. I spent most of my life in the inner city till I was 12 years old when we moved into the south central of Missouri Oxark's. For me it felt surreal, being in the country after a 12 year old life-time in a concrete jungle. As a child of the city, you were always afraid to walk alone at night. We carried weapons, travelled in groups for protection, had escape routes planned out where we could disappear fast in miles and miles of what seemed to me to be endless humanity. Then, at 12 years old, that all changed. I felt safe walking old country roads at night. Houses could be 2 or 3 miles apart instead of cramped and packed in together. You could walk all night and never see anyone. At School my older brother and I made friends with some neighbours about three miles from us. My older brother was more friendly with Bruce, who was more his age, and I made friends with Paul, he being more my age.

One Saturday, I got bored and decided to walk to my

friend's house, which I didn't do much cause it was a long walk, but off I went, and when I get there my older brother is already there talking to Bruce who is obviously still in a state of shock and fear by the look on his face. He told us; "Something followed me last night while I was walking home. I thought it was a squirrel at first, then it came closer, got heavier, like a cow, then even closer and heavier. It kept pace with me through the woods till I came to a field and I thought I'd die when it would show itself but, there was nothing to see. It's still next to me only 10-20 feet away but, there's nothing to see and this thing must be as big as an Elephant by now." I remember thinking OMG I hope that never happens to me, and the look of fear on Bruce's face haunted me anytime I walked dark country roads after that.

In time however I forgot about it, walking county roads at night (when I had to) was peaceful, relaxing. I enjoyed the solitude. Then, one night, fifteen years later in 1985, when I'm 27 years old, it happened to me. I had an old beat-up pick-up truck that I only used for short trips because it had a tendency to fail me on occasion and I'd have to leave it on the side of the road till the next day when It would decide It would serve me once again and start back up and run just fine. About three miles from my house was an all-night truck stop called the Oasis which had gotten honourable mention in the Garth Brooks song "Friends in Low Places" and I had gone there to meet a friend that never showed, so, I left there about 3 a.m. About half a mile from there my old truck once again failed me. No big deal, I'm only three miles from home, so I leave it where it stalled and start walking.

It was one of those nights when the moonshine is so bright you can see your own shadow and can see for miles. About five minutes after I start walking it started. Quiet at first, it starts deep in a thick of woods and its keeping pace with me, which unnerves me. During the day it would have been hard to keep pace in the tangle of woods, but, at night would be impossible, it made me aware that this was unnatural, whatever this was whether squirrel or deer, should not be able to keep pace with me like this at night. It very quickly started coming closer through the woods and I became aware that this (thing) was bipedal, walking on two feet, as it came closer. I move to the other side of the road and keep my eyes on the woods as I walk.

Up ahead around a bend in the road is a field that someone had bulldozed a section of woods into a deep hollow at the far end of the field. As I come to this clearing I tell myself that whatever this is will be plain to see in the moonlight once it's out of the wood's and it'll be something I should have known or expected would be there and I'd feel silly that I, a grown man, had been afraid in the first place. But, from the sounds it made in the woods, I knew that was not going to happen. Situations like this make a person cast about for a reason. You tell yourself that it's anything except what you can see or hear (or not see). However, when I did come to the clearing it got worse. It came closer, was louder, from the sound it made; It must be a couple ton's. I'd heard cattle run before, and they make a heavy sound from their weight, but this was much heavier, and like I've said, bipedal.

Now it's out in the open and I still can't see whatever this is. I'm on the far side of the road and this is from what I can hear no more then thirty feet away, just on the other side of the fence and I should be able to see something, but, there's just this LOUD thumping sound It makes as It walks next to me. If I walk faster, It walks faster, If I slow, It slows, If I stop, It stops. I then remember back all those years ago of the look of fear on my friend Bruce's face and how I'd felt dread that such a thing should ever happen to me, and now I'm thinking, this is real, this is happening.

By now the fear is so palpable. If I'd had a knife I could have cut you off a piece and handed it to you, but, in spite of instinct to run, I keep a façade of calm and just walk, running would give whatever this was reason to give chase. I keep walking by force of will and keep my eyes on the field next to me and my sights on the brush pile at the end of the half-mile long field, there are whole trees in that pile and it's twice as high as my house; whatever this was had to stop once I got there. But, it didn't. It just kept on going straight through the brush pile tearing up country as it did. Now, I could try and explain the sound of a five ton spook tearing through brush but there's just no way to describe It. POW, POP, SNAP. Still not good enough. But, I will tell you this, once and once only. I screamed, like a school girl and took off running. I've never done that before you know, screamed in fear I mean.

It stands to reason that it must have stopped following me, I mean, I'm still here, but, I don't remember the run the rest of the way home. I don't think I was abducted or anything like that, my opinion is that I was fear blanked. This is no-where near the end of this story. I've talked to several people with similar stories of what I think is this same creature that I now call stick man. A couple months after my encounter I was talking to my brother and told him what had happened and half expected him to call bull..., cause that's how he is, one of those people that doesn't believe in anything. Anyway, he told me that around the same time (different night) he and his friend Steve were sitting on the hood of their car down by the Gasgonade river which is just outside our town and near where I'd had my scare, when they started to notice that they were hearing a noise across the river on the other side of a field that was next to the one were I'd had my scare.

He said it started up top of a wooded hill about a half mile from where they sat. It was loud enough that they could hear it from that distance as it came down the hill and into an open field and continued toward them, getting louder all the way the whole time and, as with me, there's nothing to see, and, like me, they can't get their heads around that fact. "We can't see anything," he told me, and from the sound of it there should be a house walking toward them. It finally crossed the field and came to the line of brush that grew along the river and tore through the brush to the river and jumped in and started toward them and the whole time, there's nothing to see even though he and his friend could see the splash It made as It swam toward them. While he was telling me this story he told me he had an overpowering urge to get in the car and beat it outta there long before It made it halfway across the field, but, being young and all that, he wasn't going to be the first to turn tail and run, not with his friend there. It was when It jumped in the water and started swimming toward them that they both lost their nerve, jumped into the car and fish tailed it outta there.

Now comes the story of Jack. Jack was a tattooed hippie type that once told me during a conversation about whatever this was that had followed me and scared my brother that he (Jack) welcomed the unknown no matter how dark. Yeah, he was a little on the scary side. We where having these conversations every morning because I was Jack's ride to work and every morning he would walk to my house have coffee and kill time till it was time to leave for work. He lived about a mile from me outside of town and sometime during the first week he started riding with me to work he just sort of mentioned in an off-hand don't care kinda way tells me: "Something followed me in the woods this morning; it does every morning."

When I ask about it he tells me basically the same story that my brother and I shared. He told me it started the first day he started walking to my house to catch a ride to work. "If I'm walking next to the field, It's in the woods. If I walk next to the wood's, It's in the field," he told me. He said It was there every morning. When I ask if he could see it, he said he thought It was hiding from him because he was trying to get a look at It. He told me; "When It's on the other side of the road in the wood's I try and surprise It and jump to the other side of the road and It appears to go into the field. Then I jump to the other side where the field is and It goes back into the wood's." It went like that for a couple months, then one morning he comes in for coffee and tells me; "I saw It. It was in the woods and when I jumped to the side of the road where It was this morning, It didn't go to the other side into the field this time. It was behind a tree and It moved so fast that it was a blur but It would stop long enough for me to get a good look at It."

Jack told me It was 8-9 feet tall and was black and

48

looked like a stick man, the kind of stick figure we used to draw as children in school. He said It moved so fast that It wavered into a blur as It moved back and forth between trees and that's what made the sound of loud walking that my brother and I had heard, then It would stop so he could see It, standing still for a few seconds, then start the blurry wavy movement again. Since then my friends and I just call It stick man. This all happened a long time ago. I don't walk county roads much these days but every once in awhile I hear some one brag that their not scared of anything and that they're gonna go out in the woods and dare any kinda bogie to show itself. My advice is, don't go, you'll find what you're looking for......'

In April 2013, John wrote an account of a very strange experience he'd had the night before. He had gone on the internet to try to find an explanation as to what it was that he had seen. He found people who had also sent in their strange encounters, and he described his, hoping someone else would recognise his experience and be able to make sense of his. He says; "I live in Northern Minnesota in a small town. I was out walking my dog on our usual route at around 9.15 pm. Out on the edge of town we usually walk over the bridge across the river and then come back over and head home. To get there we turn at an intersection with some street lights behind us.

As we're approaching the intersection, a tall silhouette figure walked very fast across it, dressed all in black and wearing what looked like a duster coat. With the lights behind me I should have been able to make out the person's face but it was like he was a silhouette. There was no detail at all.

It seemed to be male but it was moving unnaturally fast toward the bridge. My dog started to get very agitated. As I looked up again, the figure had reached the bridge, and it seemed to turn and look at us but I can't be sure. How fast it had reached the bridge and yet it had made no sound. It's a quiet spot – I should have heard footsteps.

I was very aware it was "aware" of us. I kept telling myself this was all in my mind and yet as I was walking closer, my alarm bells were going off. I've been training in martial arts for the past thirty or so years; I also teach students defence tactics; but, my training has taught me if it feels wrong, it is. I turned 180 and started walking away. I swear I could feel it's stare on my back as I walked away. It was so intense that I couldn't help but look back around to make sure it wasn't moving up behind me.... I have to admit I am still uneasy about this situation....'

A lady called Sarah writes, on thespiritseekers wordpress; *"I live in the Forest of Dean (in the county of Gloustershire, England) and I was walking my dog through the woods the other day in a remote place that is full of ancient caves called Devils Chapel. It was raining and we had just reached a part where the path gets narrow when suddenly I saw this figure standing in the path next to a tree. It was solid black, like a silhouette. It's arms were as if had hands resting on hips but it looked just like a Lowry drawing. It felt like it was a warning not to go any farther -we didn't! - opting instead for running very fast back the way we had come! I would have put it down to imagination had my dog not gone running up to it with her tail wagging and head up looking towards where it's face should have been.*

And yet, maybe these things are not always dark? *Taishi described an experience that happened in November 2014, just before 9 pm when out with their dog. It was their dog that saw it first. "A 7-9 foot white figure creeping behind a tree, snapping a branch on the floor..."*

What are these entities, and what do they want with us?

Chapter 3: Strange Sightings

Recently, I received some correspondence from a man called Jamie.

'My name is Jamie, and I just finished reading your book 'Taken in the Woods,' and I wanted to share these two particular harrowing accounts concerning the same stretch of forest. The stretch of woods is part of what's known as Wayne National Forest which stretches across three counties of southern Ohio: Lawrence, Scioto, and Jackson counties. The encounter took place on a trail that borders Lawrence and Scioto counties.

During the summer of 1993, me and a friend sighted a very strange creature in the woods of southern Ohio. I'll call him "Bill" for the sake of this story. It was an evening in June of 1993, and me and my friend "Bill" decided to do some fishing in some old strip mining lakes located in Wayne National Forest (Scioto County), Ohio. Very beautiful country, by the way. The lakes were located in a clearing on a hilltop in the middle of the forest. We parked on the side of the paved road, grabbed our gear, took ATV trails from the main road about three miles west through thick forest, and reached the clearing and lakes. It made for a great afternoon.

Needles to say, the night descended upon us before we knew it. I voiced my concerns, but "Bill" being very familiar with the terrain, was confident in getting us back. Fortunately, the moon was bright that night, and the way back was easily navigated. The scene was beautiful. About a mile into the moonlit forest, "Bill" stopped talking and pointed over my left shoulder into the woods, and whispered "Look at that." I turned, and about a fifty yards off to my left was some type of animal. 'Bill' told me it was probably a wild cat, and continued onwards. I was a bit nervous and kept eyeing the creature that was following us. I never encountered a wild cat in the woods before, and intended to move on, and get away from it as fast as I could. I bolted, and the supposed 'wild cat' paced us with each step. I thought that kind of odd, and so did "Bill." We knew something wasn't normal.

This is where it gets really weird. When we stopped, the creature stopped, and now it was a little closer. And it appeared bigger than any wild cat I'd heard ever seen in books or at a zoo. 'Bill' agreed. Not only did it stop, but it rose up on two feet, and looked in our direction. Both 'Bill' and I thought, "Oh crap, a bear!" But it didn't have dark fur. The fur was white or a light color. I was a little freaked by this time, and Bill pointed out something. This creature was mimicking our movements. And it did! To test this, Bill waved, and it waved. Then I waved, and it waved. By this time, we were both freaked out, and we ran. It got on all fours, paced us, getting a little closer. Again, it stopped when we did and rose on two feet again.

This thing had to be at least seven to eight feet tall when it stood up, and covered in grayish-white hair. And we really couldn't make out facial features that well. I mean, it seemed like there were two dark spots where eyes should be, but that was all we could make out. I'd never been so scared in my life. I thought we were both in big trouble. Both of us broke into a sprint, and didn't stop until we were at the edge of the woods and onto the main road, not far from the car. We looked back the way we'd come and the creature had gone. The creature was nowhere to be seen. It had disappeared.

Several weeks later, we returned to that fishing spot, but there was no sign of the creature. And we continued fishing there, but never saw it again after that. I'll never forget the experience we had that night.

Here's the second part of that story:My wife and I began dating the summer of 1994, and I made the decision of taking her to the same fishing spot my friend Bill and I went to the previous summer. She agreed.So in July of 1994, a year after my first harrowing experience in that stretch of forest, I made the decision to go back out there, but this time without my trusty guide and good friend, 'Bill.' And we'd been out there several times since with no incidents, and no more creature sightings. And I just knew I would have no problem getting me and my wife back safely. Hmmm...famous last words.

We set out in early afternoon with fishing gear and our back packs that contained snacks, water bottles, flashlights, and lighters. We had a great day, but sure enough time got away from us. And that's the weird thing about this particular piece of land, time seemed to pass at such a rapid pace, or you just seemed to lose track of time.

Anyway, rain clouds moved in and dusk was upon us. We decided to head out before we were caught in the rain. I got us onto the trail back, and darkness descended and the wind picked up. We turned on our flashlights and continued on the trail. It ended in a small clearing; it was more like a field surrounded by trees. Neither one of us recalled this area. We attempted to locate the trail head we'd taken and could not. It's as if the trail had changed. Then it started to rain.

Eventually we did find an ATV trail, but it wasn't the same one we'd taken in. The rain increased to a shower, and our flashlights died. We took out our lighters, cupped them in our hands, and one at a time, they both lost their flints. I know, this sounds so cliché, but this is how it happened. The ATV trail became deep grooved ATV tracks, and we began to stumble and fall. It was excruciating. We were miserable. And I made a horrible decision. I decided to blindly take us off the trail, into the woods, and go as the crow flies. Ugh... I know... stupid decision.

Oh, we wandered in the woods for what seemed like an hour, and the rain stopped, the sky cleared, and again a bright moon lit our way. It was eerily like the night my friend Bill and I saw the creature. I was freaked out.

My soon-to-be wife saw something on the forest floor over my shoulder. I spun around and saw something white on the ground about twenty paces away. The first thing I thought was, oh crap, its bones, and we continued onward until we came to the odd sight.

On the ground at our feet, was an arrow made of pure white stones. I got down and touched them with my fingertips. They were cut and laid in the ground with precision. And they seemed to be limestone or marble....maybe. I couldn't be sure. They were very smooth, and this was freaking me out. The hair on my neck rose. I got the feeling of being watched, and my memory of the previous summer came rushing back. My wife suggested we follow the arrow, which was pointing to the left. My gut reaction was 'Hell No!' She then asked, "Well, what the hell are we gonna do? We're lost, its night, and we have to do something."

Panic was beginning to seep in. But I kept it together, and I made a very odd decision that may have very well saved both out lives. I decided we go in a ninety degree angle from the arrow. Up, instead of following it left. We headed in a straight line upwards from the arrow, through the woods about twenty feet, and came out onto the two lane paved road. We realized from surrounding landmarks that we were about a half mile down the hill from our car. We were never more happy to be alive, and we never returned to those woods after that.

To this day, it still seems that particular trail changed after nightfall. I do know I'll never forget that feeling of fear, and my instinctive reaction to not follow that white arrow in the ground. Was someone or something trying to help us or lure us somewhere? And what made me instinctively not follow that arrow, but go in a direction away from it? These are still questions that come to mind after all these years....

~ ~ ~

Another baffling story comes from a couple in Texas; 'Our story (only one of many) involves 2 of our dogs....German Shepherds, (brother and sisters, 4 years old at the time.)We had purchased a VERY remote cabin in the Ozarks near Eureka Springs, AR. 3 years ago, deep in a wooded area on top of a mountain, very inaccessible by car (even with 4wheel drive) or foot. We had only one neighbor, quite distant and our acreage of 45 acres was surrounded on three sides by natural park land. Our dogs had a lot of freedom to run and play, but always under our supervision due to the presence of many large wild animals (wolves, bear, wild hogs, mountain lions) and we were always armed with a gun when they (or we) were outside the house.....a very rugged and untamed area - and to me anyway, frightening and forbidding.

There is also a huge cavern running under the property. On three occasions, at dusk, these two German Shepherds ran to the top of a rocky ridge at the edge of the cleared "yard" area, 250 yards from the cabin and disappeared through the forest and over the edge, down the mountainside, while we were screaming for them to come back. The weather would turn very stormy/cold following these disappearances, and we could not follow them anyway because of the density of the woods. Each time, they re-appeared after 2 days (of wet weather). They would come up to the long covered front porch (18 feet off the ground, 11 steps up) and scratch on the door.

Here is the very strange thing: after two days and three nights of being out in the wild, they would return in a DRY, pristine condition; no wet, tangled fur, no mud on feet or bodies, no burrs, leaves, or forest "stuff" on them at all!! -These are LONG-HAIRED Shepherds- everything gets in their fur. It was like they had been picked up and carried! And the cave has a very damp and muddy floor; no way they had been in there...but where DID they go???

These are obedient, well-trained dogs whose siblings are all police service animals. They do NOT disobey-until they got to that mountain! We sold the cabin soon after; our dogs are like family and these "vanishings" unnerved us. This spot is eerie and lonely enough to make a person edgy and uncomfortable anyway....I promise you that there is something very wrong here....I never went out after dark. And these dogs have never run away again.

You tell me what caused these dogs to leave or; who sheltered them??? We remain puzzled....the dogs ran over the ridge and never looked back with any hesitation....and the weather followed the disappearances, not preceded. The house sits on an old Civil War camp-ground, and was also a Native American spot. (Possibly pre-historic native people's too).

My wife had some experiences inside the cabin-one night. She got up to go to the bathroom (I was not there) and when she returned 3 minutes later, there was a brand new comforter on the bed! She was constantly hearing low sounds of conversations outside the house; laughter, singing and talking, all on an almost sub-audible, murmuring level. She had to have white noise (2 fans) in the bedroom at night to try and block it out. She also saw lights moving through the forest at night. We put up heavy drapes to block this. All in all, a very spooky place. We live now in a remote wooded area of north-east Texas.

~ ~ ~

Recently, a gentleman called Luke contacted me with a series of very strange incidents that he'd experienced in the outback, in the Northern Territory of Australia.

'I live in Australia and I've spent most of my life in the bush and deep outback, working as a remote area surveyor for mining companies and in various roles in remote Aboriginal communities, particularly in Arnhemland in the Northern Territories. I would describe myself as having a healthy dose of scepticism but like many, I would love to see proof of paranormal or the supernatural - I'm just yet to be convinced of any particularly specific phenomena. That said, I consider myself first and foremost a bushman - I hunt, hike, scout etc... almost every day, and I can safely say that although I can't begin to explain it or offer up any new hypothesis, there is definitely more going on in the woods than we can currently explain by conventional means. I have had the 'watched' feeling many times, as well as experienced the "vacuum" of no sound and an almost physical detachment many people describe, while by myself in the bush.

I can relate to you a couple of specific odd events, and I'll start with my experiences in the Upper Murray area of Northeast Victoria/Southeast New South Wales. I leased a hundred acres of old growth bush off my uncle when I was in my early 20's, and moved into the rough, off-grid shack on it with my girlfriend. Water wheel for 12v lighting and an old car stereo wired in for music and that was it. Rustic but I liked it. The block rose steadily towards the back boundary, and was surrounded by a National Park of very old, very thick sub-alpine bush. We enjoyed the simple life immensely, and I hunted at least twice a week to supplement our meat.

Anyway, the hundred acres had two clearings on it, both about ten acres. One was the 'House Paddock' in a creek valley, and the other was at the top of the rise adjoining the back boundary, unused and surrounded by windrows; I'll call this the Back Paddock for clarity. There was very thick bush between the House Paddock and the Back Paddock, with a central track joining the two (too overgrown to drive but clearly defined) and another track we'll call the Side Track that ran parallel to the western boundary of the whole property, including alongside the Back Paddock and to a gate that led into the National Park. The whole boundary of the hundred acres was well fenced, but the two clearings were not fenced internally. Essentially, the only fencing was the boundary and a small fence around the house itself.

One afternoon I decided to walk along the Side Track to the Back Paddock to see if I could see any kangaroos grazing on the wild grasses that grew there. I wandered through the bush along the track - very familiar with my surroundings as I knew every inch of the hundred acres - and began to slow down and stalk as I got closer to the Back Paddock. Sure enough there were a couple of roos grazing and I quickly took my shot. I heard my shot hit (it's a distinct hollow thump when you hit an animal's body) but the roo jumped away behind a windrow. I knew my shot was good and it couldn't have got far. There was blood on the grass and a clear trail of flattened grass leading from where I had shot the roo to behind the windrow. There was no sign of the roo at all, though. I began to doubt my accuracy and feel guilty that I had wounded an animal and it was now dying slowly somewhere in pain. I never take a shot unless I'm sure, but no one is perfect, right? I began to cast around for tracks and signs to find it, but there was nothing. I walked all the way around the windrow and then stopped dead when I saw the carcass of the roo laying on top of MY trail that I had made when I'd crossed the windrow, right near the blood stains where my bullet had hit it. That was a bit weird, but perhaps it had looped around behind me when it heard me coming around the windrow and then finally died back in the open.

As I approached it, things got really strange. There was still grass in it's mouth, as if it had died instantly still chewing when I shot it. This didn't make sense. A wounded animal would surely spit out it's meal when fleeing, or it would fall out during it's last moments of gasping (sorry for the graphic nature of this tale, but I need to be detailed as you'll soon see). The roo appeared to have died instantly where it was. I figured maybe I had watched another roo escape around the side of the windrow, and somehow walked past the dead one without seeing it. I really tried my hardest to rationalise it. I felt it's body and it was still warm but - bizarrely - I discovered it's fur was saturated. It seemed to have been in the rain or had a dunk in a pond. The afternoon was cool but dry, and I couldn't account for this. I started to dress the carcass, skinning it quickly. I then realised I couldn't find a bullet hole anywhere in the carcass. No damaged organs, no bleeds, no holes in the hide which I had removed and checked on both sides (flesh side and fur side). I was a bit unnerved now, and decided to leave the meat. It was just too weird to risk eating it. Perhaps a roo had died of a disease just before I got to the Back Paddock and I'd walked past it in my haste to follow the other roo behind the windrow and now was just confusing this carcass for a roo that had indeed escaped wounded. It was getting dark and I decided to head back home and write it off as weird coincidence, although I felt really guilty about possibly wounding an animal and allowing it to escape.

I crossed the clearing and started heading for the Central Track that would get me home a bit quicker than the Side Track. Then, things got... really odd. There was suddenly no sound at all - a vacuum had descended, as such - and I had a horrible feeling I was being scrutinised malevolently. It was stomach-churning. I then began to notice that the Central Track didn't look right. It was wider, somehow, and more overgrown. The trees seemed to close in on it more, and overhung it, giving the illusion of walking into a tunnel. It wasn't usually like that. It was just an old track. It was also more...verdant. That's the only way I can describe it. It was so green it was like a jungle, and it seemed to glow despite the descending rapid dusk. I hurried along it, sure I was being followed, ducking under

branches and squeezing past boughs that I had never noticed before. Usually, you could walk this track at a casual stroll. Now, I was having to almost fight my way along. I should have reached the creek and crossed into the House Paddock in about ten minutes, but I stumbled along for ages, at least a half hour, and it became true night. I was, frankly, near cra....g myself.

I knew if I kept going downhill I'd have to reach the creek or at worst the boundary fence very soon - but I knew in my gut I should have come across either well and truly already. I followed that track for TWO HOURS, and getting desperate, I remembered a silly folklore thing my Grandma told me about fairies when I was a kid - that they would seek to get you lost in the woods, and if you turned your coat inside out and put it back on they may let you go. So, that's what I did. I put my shirt on inside out and fired three shots into the air - a signal I had with my neighbors if any of us were in trouble. I'd actually already fired off shots in a panic, but no-one had replied. About five minutes after reversing my shirt I stepped straight off a bank and into the creek. I could hear crickets and a boobook owl and I'd never been so happy to slip on my arse into the water. I also noticed it was actually still only dusk, and was not nearly as dark as it had appeared in the trees. I crossed the creek and fully expected to come out into the House Paddock - I'd see the house lights any minute. I didn't though. Instead I walked into a clearing in a pine plantation I recognised, about eight kilometres from my property. I was utterly dumbfounded. I had somehow crossed our boundary without climbing the fence, and even though I'd been walking south and downhill, I'd come out 8km to the West - UPHILL from my place.

I walked home and just in time to find my girlfriend, my uncle and my neighbor all preparing to come looking for me as I was always home before dark and they had started to worry - enough so that my girlfriend had rang my uncle and neighbour saying she had a "bad feeling". I couldn't account for the time differences - I had been walking for hours but was only about 40 minutes overdue - or for the distances I'd covered so I kept it to myself. Interestingly, no one had heard my rifle shots at all. I have absolutely no explanation for any of this - I put my shirt on backwards because I was desperate and panicky, not because I believed I was being harassed by fairies. Still...

A couple of other things happened in the same area. I've added you on Facebook, so you can see I'm a relatively normal (admittedly foul-mouthed and over-opinionated) dude who doesn't really go in for much of this stuff - I think most people are kidding about their weird encounters, to be honest. I'm also quite disliked in certain cryptozoology circles because I run a tracking education group and regularly debunk supposed puma, thylacine, and yowie "evidence" by objectively analysing the tracks and almost always revealing them to be dog, dog, and human respectively. I have a reputation as a sceptic.'

The other stuff that happened on the same property; When I was around 16 or so, I was staying at the shack with my uncle, aunt, and cousin. One morning my cousin, who was around 14, was mucking about on the wooded hillside opposite the house, about 100 metres from where we were sitting on the verandah drinking coffee and watching him idly. He seemed to be sneaking/stalking up on something, and it was quite amusing to watch him crawling and sneaking from tree to tree. Eventually he made his way back to us and seemed really, really surprised to see me sitting there.

He swore that a large, dark, man was sneaking around him in the trees, and he had presumed it was me as I'm 6'5" and often played tricks on him. At the time I owned a camouflaged jacket and he said that I must have been wearing it and that's why he couldn't make me out properly. His uncle and aunt confirmed I had been with them the whole time and that we'd watched him sneaking along trying to catch "it"/me, but he wasn't having it. It freaked the hell out of me. To this day he still thinks we played a trick on him.

This was on the same hillside as the experience I told you about earlier, right on the edge of the House Paddock.

Another one, everyone including myself was pretty drunk, so grain of salt and all that. My uncle, my semi-hermit neighbor (he lived up on that hillside in a little cabin made of cargo pallets and bred guinea pigs to eat. Yes!...) and my girlfriend were all partying in the shack, drinking and playing guitar and such. Well into the night my uncle went outside to "get some fresh air" (to vomit). He was gone for ages and I staggered out to look for him. He wasn't on the verandah so I searched around the yard for him in the moonlight. Then, I swear I saw him on the roof. It was a single span roof, not an a-frame, by the way. It was his silhouette, just standing on the edge, hands on hips. There was a small glow where his mouth would be and I took it to be a cigarette.

I called up to him to come down but he ignored me, standing just like a statue. I kept talking, telling him he'd hurt himself and to get down etc... A window slid open and my girlfriend asked from inside what I was yelling about and I told her my uncle had climbed up on the roof for some reason. She pointed out how odd it was we hadn't heard him climb up. I used the window cill to boost myself up and I could get my eyes just above the roof-line. The silhouette was now on the other side of the roof. I hadn't heard it step on the tin at all. I dropped back to the ground, mumbled something to my girlfriend about climbing up to get him down, and headed to the water tank stand, by which I'd be able to clamber up onto the roof. I kept my eyes on the silhouette the whole time, and only took them off for a second while I climbed up onto the edge of the stand. It was gone, though. I climbed back down, fairly disconcerted, and went back to the verandah. Eventually my uncle appeared, dishevelled and wet and dirty. He'd walked down into the creek gully and slipped in, then lay on the bank to recover. He could hardly walk and was in no condition to be climbing on any roof.'

I was intrigued by the dark figure seen on the roof, and the figure his cousin had thought was him, stalking him. I asked Luke, "Did it seem to look like a solid shape? Could it have been the same thing, on both occasions?" "Yeah, it was definitely solid, the shape I saw on the roof. It blocked out the stars from view. I always had the gut feeling it was the same "thing", whatever it is. It was certainly an odd place. I never felt a real sense of malevolence, but the time I got "lost" still gives me the heebie jeebies. My cousin described the thing he saw as "big, dark and dappled-looking." I guess the "dappled" thing was why he thought it was a camouflaged jacket, which I guess it still could have been (just not mine...) He said it was ducking from bush to bush and tree trunk to tree trunk, like it was trying to hide or sneak up on him."

I asked him, "If you could put a label on it, what would you say you think it could have been? ie spirit, demonic....or ... ? "Maybe something else entirely. Elemental or something. An interesting side note is the story my uncle told me one night when the subject of UFOs and ghosts and the like came up while we were driving a lonely back-road. He is an immensely practical man, and one of the last true bushmen (he hunts wild pigs for a living and has also worked in forestry). He does not exaggerate, brag, or tell tall tales. He is what I would consider to be honest to a fault. He is also quite guarded. I was really surprised when he opened up and told me he had had an intense series of out-of-body experiences or lucid dreams, while living at the aforementioned property. They started with him suddenly becoming aware he was "drifting up" as he dozed, and then seeing himself in bed. The first time he said he visited a pine plantation he once worked in, and then other locations nearby.

During one of the experiences, though, he said he encountered three "very old" beings (he got the sense they were very old men, but not men) who told him they wanted him to go with them for some task of undefined but monumental importance, as they were no longer strong enough to complete the task. He said he did not feel threatened - in fact he said they seemed "nice", but he got the feeling if he went with them he'd be under their control and would be "swept along". He told them he'd go with them if they allowed him to "drive" - as in he'd follow them but retain control of his movements. They said this wasn't possible so he decided not to follow them. He said he encountered the beings on two other occasions but didn't offer any further details. I was gob-smacked he'd told me, and with the matter of fact way he told it.

I'll tell you about some of the weird stuff I saw up in Arnhemland when I worked in Aboriginal communities. There's some high strangeness in those places at times. The Yolngu folk are still living a semi-tribal life, and they are deeply superstitious and have strong beliefs in spirits and magic. The communities are a hotbed of gossip and suspicion at times. Gulka, or black magic, is greatly feared. When you live amongst it for a long time it's contagious. There is definitely some weird telepathy going on in some Aboriginal communities. Like a Hive Mind, almost. For instance, you'll think about someone you haven't seen in ages, or even just get an intense sudden thought about someone, and then they appear. That hivemind thing in Aboriginal communities, I've never had it anywhere else. I'm the most un-psychic person ever. But I've discussed it with both blackfellas and whitefellas who lived in communities and many have reported similar sensations. And they do have shapechanger legends. Gulkamen (evil sorcerers) can supposedly change themselves into snakes and dingoes.

In Arnhemland I lived in a community called Gapuwiyak in 2007 and worked for the local council. This place is really remote and right on the edge of the Arafura swamp, which is pretty much a no- man's land. Anyway, my crew had the job of seeding and trying to get grass to grow on a new football oval that the community was pretty excited for (a lot of remote communities exist on the poverty line and have very little in the way of stuff for kids to do etc... and Aboriginal people tend to unanimously love their football). It was the Dry Season, and we were pushing to get the grass established before the monsoon came and washed all the seed away, so we were watering it 24/7 with these big sprinklers that pulled themselves along on a cable. Every six hours or so we had to move the sprinklers and run out the cable again. I lived right next to the oval and volunteered to do the midnight sprinkler run. I took a torch and walked out onto the edge of the oval. There was no moon and it was REALLY dark.

In most Aboriginal communities there are packs of half-feral dogs that people call "Camp Dogs". Some of them have owners but a lot don't, and even the ones that do are often neglected. It's depressing but that's another story (one of my dogs is a rescued camp dog. She's so sweet natured it breaks my heart to think about the life her brothers and sisters must have lived). Anyway, these camp dogs form packs and hang around scavenging what they can. They can be savage (the blackfellas call the mean ones "cheeky dogs") and Gapuwiyak in particular had some nasty packs. So while I was standing there on the edge of the oval shining my torch around, a pack of dogs appeared out of the dark, yipping and growling and carrying on. They sort of surrounded me but didn't really attack. I told them to p... off and kicked at them a bit but they wouldn't leave me alone. It was extra weird because they seemed to be blocking me from walking out onto the oval, but if I walked back to my house for a bit they flanked me but let me go. When I'd head towards the edge of the oval again they would nip at my legs and bark and run around and around me. I eventually got annoyed and chased them off by throwing rocks. They retreated but watched me from the edge of the oval as I walked out towards the first sprinkler.

I set it up again and moved onto the second. Suddenly, from a house nearby, I could hear several people singing in Yolngu Matha, the local aboriginal language. It was an urgent, emotional kind of singing and I've only heard something with a similar mood at funeral ceremonies. I thought it was odd, but Aboriginal people are often up very late playing cards and hanging out so I figured they were just practising for a ceremony or something. I set up the next sprinkler and walked back towards my house. As soon as I was off the oval the dogs joined me again, and trotted along with me until I was at my gate. I couldn't hear the singing anymore as I went inside and thought nothing else of it until I saw one of the old ladies, Joyce, who lived in the house the singing was coming from.

I told her I'd heard their song the night before and asked why they were up so late singing. She said "There was a Mukay on the oval last night. The wartu (dogs) were scared of it and barking." A Mukay is sort of a generic term for an evil spirit. It's pronounced "mook-oi-ee". I laughed a bit, and assured her that it was only me on the oval and the dogs were barking at me. She shook her head and said: "No. We saw you. The Mukay was coming for YOU. The wartu were trying to tell you. You still walked out there so we sang that Mukay away for you. It was going to get you." I lost my smug grin pretty quick after that.

Chapter 4: Stalked

I was recently contacted by a young man called Séamus who lives in Ireland and grew up in a small rural village called Ferns in County Wexford. Ferns was established in the 6th Century and was home to the Kings of Ireland.

"It all sounds so outlandish that quite a few years have passed and I've only ever told a handful of people who I trusted enough not to judge me, you know?" Séamus had contacted me after hearing me on a radio show describing some people's experiences of hearing disembodied screams or wailing in the Woods, with no logical reason as to why they were hearing it or where it was coming from. The wailing type-thing happened three times when I was 11, and a fourth when I was 17, and I remember them each clearly. It was 1996, I had a good group of friends, two of them were in my class and it was the summer just before we were heading into secondary school. Another friend was a year above us, already in high school and lastly a younger pal who was two years below in my younger sister's class. All that summer we spent our nights camping out, literally as many nights a week as we could. Like I said, I grew up in a small village so I guess our parents felt safe enough letting us do so back then. There was a field, said to be haunted and we pitched a tent there. Nothing happened the first or second night, then on the third night the field was engulfed in a thick fog. There was a full moon.

I remember we were in the middle of the field and the fog just kept getting closer to our little camp-site, and in the fog, sitting bright in the moon-light was the shape of a house at the bottom of the field, where there was definitely no house. We couldn't figure it out, so we left the field and decided to venture off into the village. It was late, the place was dead quite, it was a ghost town and we thought this was great. It became a habit; we would pitch a tent in one of our yards and when everyone was asleep we would go around the village looking for spooky things, smoking cigarettes we stole from our parents thinking we were the bee's knees!

STALKED IN THE WOODS

So one night, we are camping in my friend Tommy's house. We were talking about where

we were going to check out, I mean there are a lot of supposed haunted spots around there, a lot of ancient medieval sites and stuff, but Tommy kept asking us to stay quiet; he was certain that he could hear something. We zipped open the tent door and stood out to have a listen. Now I'll just try quickly to explain the layout a little. At the back of Tommy's house, and in fact at the back of all the houses along that the row, there is a large field. To the left of the field is a narrow road called the 'Station Road'. Now going up along Station Road, if you take a left turn, it leads to the road that Tommy's house is situated on. If you continue past the turn for Tommy's, on up the station road maybe 500 meters, there is a turn off for my estate. Continue further, maybe only another 500 meters, maybe less, you enter the main street in the village. There is a right and left turn here; the right will bring you onto the main road leading straight outside the village to Camolin, the left will bring you into the bottom of the village. Mentioning this is necessary.

So there we were, standing outside the tent, looking in toward the field at the back of Tommy's. At first we needed a little convincing, but when we actually took notice we could hear a faint sound coming from what seemed like pretty far down the station road. But it starts getting closer, and closer and soon it was pretty damn high up the road. Steph it is difficult to describe it; it sounded soft, like a woman not moaning but, I dunno, and it was constant, there was no pause for breath. It went higher up the road then stopped. We were afraid it was going to come across the field so we scrabbled into the tent. There was a metal swinging gate leading down to the back. We heard this being opened. To the left of the tent was a large pigeon hutch that Tommy's father had, it was a load of old school shelves really. To the right was a shed where at night they would lock the dog inside.

Almost instantly after we heard the gate open, the dog began to snarl and growl and then the pigeons went nuts, flying and cooing, then they were soon gone and the dog just shut up completely; then someone kept walking around the tent, even hitting off of it at one point, and I have to be honest what happened next I think I blocked out of my mind because I can only remember us all huddled side by side face down on the ground, and I think we may have been crying but after that it's a blank, I think I must have just cried myself to sleep.

A couple of weeks later, Tommy, and a guy named Thom who sadly is not with us anymore, (Thom's parents were the owners of a shop/chippy at the bottom part of the village.) The boys had planned to sneak out of their houses on a particular night. I was still nervous from the night in the tent, but when 3 a.m. came, they were firing chippings at my window and I reluctantly snuck out to meet them.

They were very jittery and said they had heard something weird, and while they were waiting for me they thought they seen a face in a van parked across from my house. We walked to the main street, turned left and headed up to the middle of the village to the church. It's high and on a bit of a hill, but the grounds are nice and open. Across from it, just a little bit up the main road on the right hand side is another estate. I remember we were smoking a fag when we heard the wailing noise again. It was back down at the bottom of the village; we were shocked, but this thing was clever. Somehow, at a pace that just would not be possible for a person, it did not come up the main street but instead went through a field, or so it seemed, and cleared this field, entered the lower end of the estate across from the church and not once did it take a breath, because it did not stop wailing. Now it was working up through Rosemary heights, the estate opposite the church, and was above us higher up the main street. It was getting so close, we ran; I am actually trembling a little now as I am writing this and feel cold spots all over me.

We ran down the road and could hear it chasing us. We ran through a side door at Thom's parent's shop and climbed up on large barrels of chip fat waste, then onto a wall and into Thom's bedroom window - this was the route he used to sneak out. We were only seconds in the bedroom, his brother was in there looking completely baffled at us, wondering why the hell we were there, just seconds in when the side door slammed open and we could here something thrashing stuff about. We would later see cardboard boxes and plastic and other stuff tossed around when it got bright. We sat there till around 7 a.m., when it was good and bright, then ran home before our parent's got up.

I heard it one more time that summer. Myself and the younger guy in the group were having a sleep over, he was not there for the first two events, and I was happy with that. It was late in the night, or actually it was early in the morning, we were playing Tekken 2 on the playstation, trying to clear the game. I was in the top of the bed and he was in the bottom when this noise that I can only describe as awful, a pure awful sound; not a soft wail, it was disgusting, loud and just I dunno, it was a sound meant to make you feel fear. I have trouble trying to replicate it, but I can never forget it. My friend Greg began to laugh; he really was just an innocent kid. I asked him; "What are you laughing at? Do you know what that is?" and he said; "It's your da snoring'" I remember saying something along the lines of, "Is my da sleeping outside?" His expression changed when he realised that the noise was right outside my bedroom window.

We put the covers over our heads, I can't remember how long it went on for, but it was very terrifying.

Over the coming years, I did something stupid to try contact the other world and I will get into that later. For now I will just end with the last time I heard it. I was 17, again it was early in the morning and I was coming back from a party. I had a good three miles to walk to get home and everything was fine. It was a nice bright morning and I never felt even a little bit uncomfortable or out of sorts. That was until I approached my house. This sensation of dread came over me, that old fear, I took my keys out and was just about to walk through my gate when that horrible moan/groan/gut twisting sound that I heard outside my window started coming from my back yard; either my yard or my neighbour's yard. There was a second where I stared down there to see where it was coming from. It was loud and close. I remember trying to put the keys in the door for what seemed like an eternity; I was fumbling because my eyes were locked on the side of the house.

I eventually got in. I slept on the floor of my parent's

room that night, a floor I would make a bed on many times over the next year. I never heard that sound again, I have no idea what it was or what could have made it. The first time we heard it at the tent we thought it was the Banshee, though I have never heard of encounters like that with her.

I know it all sounds completely crazy. It kind of feels relieving to put it all into words, even though I have completely creeped myself out reliving it. It is kind of surreal that I kept them to myself (for the most part) for that long. It must just be the right time for them to be told. As for the rest of the story; I'll take it right back to the start where it all kicked off; my friends and I were complete idiots, plain and simple. A girl who was a good few years older than us, (I was 13 at the time,) showed us how to make a Ouija board out of a piece of paper and a coin. We thought it was great, and we pretty much got a response straight away. I'd had the previous experiences and the other lads had heard plenty of stories; we loved horror movies and heavy metal was our music of choice so we were full on 'yes let's talk to ghosts'.

We would do it anywhere we could in the village. The village has a massive historic back-story of its own; it has an old abbey that was savaged by Vikings and a Castle that was the home place of Diarmuid MacMurrough who at the time was the High King of Ireland, and believe it or not this sleepy little backward village was once the capital of Ireland some 900 years ago. So we would go to these places thinking we would surely get a response, and we did, but funnily enough we never had a response from somebody who had died during the age these constructs were in use. It was always someone from recent times. Most often, a cousin of mine who had passed away only a few years before.

The more we messed around with the board though, the stranger things got, the more aggressive things got. One night, myself, my cousin Martin and our friend Arthur were down at mine. I was babysitting, something I had to do frequently on the weekends (the joys of being the oldest of the siblings). We thought yeah we'll smoke some fags and do the Ouija board, as ya do when you're a foolish child. It started off as my cousin, then moved on to different names, one being 'Hitler' - apparently, then someone else, someone dark and mean and no matter how hard we tried, we could not get rid of the thing from the board. You see, the girl who showed us how to make this, made it very, very clear that when you are finishing with it and want to say goodbye, you absolutely must slide the coin down along the 'GOODBYE' part that is wrote down along the right side of the page. If you just get up and walk away or simply say goodbye and do not move the coin where it is supposed to be moved, then whoever you are talking to is set free. Well, we shoved and pushed against that coin as hard as we could; it wouldn't budge. We were panicking, and sure enough my parents pulled in the yard and unlocked the front door and we had no choice but to get up from the page and throw it in the fire. We thought we had made a right bollox of things and set something free.

But, a few years later I realised or at least came to believe that the board was a load of rubbish; that we were not contacting spirits via a piece of paper and a coin, naturally, but whatever was communicating was already there, it was simply using the page as a means to communicate and have a little fun with us, or me. I believe that this is the reason it was my cousin who would always come through; he was one of the only people I personally knew at that time who had ever perished, so he was a natural name to use in tricking me, if that makes sense? So onto the occurrences. I can clearly remember about 5 or 6 definite things that have always stuck with me.

It all really took off around this time and continued for about four years. During that period, there was my old friends who I mentioned during the message about camping out and will mention again in the early happenings here, and who I would eventually drift away from, as you do with moving in different circles in school and whatnot, guess it just happens over time. There was also the newer friends who were equally as freaked out by my house as the previous. My house was always the place where everyone slept over, my folks were always sound that way. I remember at night the guys would not want to go downstairs on their own and were even afraid going to the toilet. My mam would often comment on my room, saying how it made her uncomfortable, especially when she was alone in the house and she had to pass by it. At one point my youngest sister, I guess this would have been late 2002, she began to mention The Man. It was bizarre seeing her focusing on something (nothing) and be very unsettled by it, something that was always on the the stairs. If the sitting room door was open, it would not be long before someone would get up and close the door because it always felt like someone was staring in from the open bars on the stairs. You couldn't walk through the house without feeling someone on top of you. I constantly had freezing cold pressure on my legs or chest any and every time I would sit down, especially when I was alone. I had sleep paralysis many times. Once in the corner of my eyes I saw a black figure sitting next to me on the bed while I tried to move or scream or just wake up.

So, I'm still 13, and still with my old pals. My cousin Martin and Greg, the young kid who had heard the noise outside my bedroom window, they were sleeping over and I was babysitting again. 'Something' hurled an action figure toy through the living room and it smacked into the aerial that was sitting on top on the television. Later that night, myself and Martin fell asleep on the couch, and when we woke up the next morning, Greg was sitting on the two- seater, his legs were up and he was pale and tired looking. He told us that when everyone had fallen asleep, he woke up to the sound of someone running up and down the stairs, and tapping the sitting-room door handle. He was too scared to move, too afraid to call us. He was terrified that if he called us and we didn't wake up, whoever was out in the hall was going to come in and get him.

Over a year later, I didn't really see either Martin or Greg much anymore. It was coming up to Christmas and Arthur was staying at my place, and again, I was babysitting. My father was in a band, always was and still is, and my mother would often go and that's how I got stuck babysitting. It took until I was 15 to get out of babysitting - and it literally took me joining my father's band! Anyway, the plan was, stay at mine then get up really early the next day and head off to Waterford on the bus and do Christmas shopping. The bus stop was closer to my house than his so it made sense. We had a fold-out couch in the kitchen so we were going to stay there. That's when we could hear someone walking around in my parent's room which was above the kitchen. The house was feeling funky at this point and he was well in the know so I asked him to come up and check it out with me, just to make sure my sisters were alright, and so I wouldn't die with fear, obviously! At the top of the stairs right in front of the top step is the bathroom, turn left and my parent's room was there, there was an open landing, small, it's an old two story council house so not a whole lot of space. To the left again then was my sisters' room, and mine.

I remember walking over to my parent's open doorway. It was black dark in there and I got so unnerved, that familiar feeling of being watched had intensified something drastic and I couldn't close the door quick enough. I went to the girls' room, opened the door and went in and made sure they were alright. They were, and they were fast asleep. So I closed the door back over and looked at Arthur; we were confused because we definitely heard someone walking about in the room above us. I went to walk back across the landing, I got to my parent's door when I swear with my hand on my heart Steph, the loudest bang came from the back of my bedroom door. It was like a sledge hammer had been hit off it. It was so loud, we ran downstairs descending it in about two steps and stood in the kitchen like two petrified dopes waiting for my parents to come home. We never mentioned it to them though; my father would not listen to stories like that let alone believe them.

Now we fast forward time to where the intense feeling in the house is in full swing. I'm 17 by now, not long after hearing that noise out in my backyard, the wailing. That year I became a little bit of a recluse, I only really went out when I was playing on the weekends with my dad's band, I stopped hanging around with the lads and I don't know why, I reckon it was a depressing side effect from the events at home.

I was lying on my sister's bed watching the television; my sisters had a TV at least three times the size of mine so I stuck a movie on in there. My legs were draped over the edge, and soon enough that cold pressure was pressing down on them. It was different this time, it wasn't just on my legs, it moved to my, manhood, we'll say and felt as though it was... I dunno.... I just had to get up and go downstairs. Later that evening I was getting a bath, I felt the same kind of interaction in there too.

Another night, I was watching the TV in my room; I always had the TV on in there and especially at night. I would never keep one in my room in my house now, but back then it was a great comfort, it had both noise and light and I needed that. I have no idea why on that occasion, I got up to go toilet and I didn't turn on my bedroom light, nor the upstairs hall light or the bathroom light, I just have no idea why because I always would have, it must have just been tiredness. The light from my TV was beaming into the hall, filling it some, but not much. It also lit up the white sink beside the toilet, and I stood there trying to pee as fast as I could whilst completely regretting not turning on the lights. A shadow passed over me and then crossed the light of the sink. Someone walked right behind me, there was a sound that I heard when it happened, like the sound of curtains being drawn fast, that for some reason is the only sound I can use to compare it to for you. I jumped and spun around, staring into the hall, it really was terrifying. But the worst was still to come.

I was down in the kitchen talking to my mother while she was making dinner. I was sitting down at the table when I felt somebody walking past me. I tried to ignore it like I usually did, but then in my hands that were cupped together under the table, I felt what I can only describe as a ball of freezing cold energy fill my hands. Inside my head I just said "f…. this," and went up to my room. This is when I decided to try and make contact.

I sat on my bed and asked out loud "Is anyone there?" I got no reply, of course, so I rattled my brain a little, then stuck my arm out and asked again, this time saying "If anyone is there, move my arm." My arm was pushed down. I was scared witless, but I was fed up of being scared witless so I just kept asking questions. "Move my arm up for yes, down for no." "Are you a boy?" "No." "Girl?" "Yes." I wanted to know her name, so I was going to say the alphabet and when I got to the first letter of her name "Move my arm." It stopped at A. Next I was going to go through a list of names beginning with A, it ended on 'Amy.'

After quite a while I found out that she died young, and that she liked being in my room, also that there were three others there. A couple who I never got names for, and a man, who I am actually getting quite nervous even thinking about. I got nervous last night too. His name was Brendan. She said he was bad.

A couple of weeks went by with this mental carry on, I was scared for obvious reasons but somewhat comforted by Amy, somehow I felt as though she would protect me now, but that wishful nonsense did not last long. I had a lamp on in my room, my TV broke; just stopped working. I would see odd shapes in the screen as it reflected my room back to me with the light of the lamp and my face would distort in it, though that could have just been pure paranoia at that point. As I lay in bed, I began to feel arms move along my legs. Every time I felt them I would spring up with fright. Eventually, I sat up on the edge of the bed and stuck my arm out. After some questions and my arm either moving up or down I found out that it was just Amy and the couple; they "apparently" wanted to just lay next to me.

I lay back down and the feeling of having arms laid across my legs happened again. It didn't feel like a full actual solid arm made of flesh and bone was there, it was more a presence, it's difficult to describe. It eventually really began to feel like there was a lot of arms there though, but the presence that seemed to be lying down by the front of my body began to seem more firm. I was lying down on my right side. I could feel the presence of someone lying at the back of my legs and an *actual* PERSON at the

STALKED IN THE WOODS

front of my legs. I froze, I could feel this figure grow, it was halfway down the bed, it felt like it had only an arm, a torso and a head but no legs, but it definitely had a head. I had my arms folded in by my chest and I will never forget this as long as I live Steph. As it grew more tangible it began to rise higher in the bed, to the point where the head was touching my elbow. I swear it had short hair, shaven, it felt rough like stubble after a man has had his head shaved with a 1 or 0 blade.

I tried to push down against it with my elbow, it felt like an hour when I think back, but it all actually happened so quick. The top of the head came out from under the blanket, I could see it, the lamp light showed it perfectly. A stubbly head was in my bed, touching my elbow. I screamed as loud as I could, jumped up from the bed holding my duvet as I did so. I start swinging it around, freaking out, just going completely nuts. My mother came to the door and I just told her to go away, I stuck my arm out and asked for Amy. Every time I asked for her my arm would spin around or it would bounce down with force. It turned out that there was no Amy, that it was this Brendan all along and for whatever reasons I'll never know he just wanted to torment me. I never tried to contact him again.

After that I made a bed on the floor in my parent's room every night for a few months and I was at my lowest point. A while back I actually asked them did they remember any of it but my Dad said it didn't happen and my mother, who I think uses forgetting as a way to deal with whatever she personally experienced herself, just said she didn't remember. That dismissive way is a killer. I would eventually get back in touch with one of my friends, I told him a little bit of what had happened and he was more than happy to let me stay in town with him, just so I could get away from Ferns and that house. But I was followed. I would feel it pushing down on the blankets at night and feel it walk behind me and watch me in the bathroom, it just never let up.

Then an aunt of mine who was going through a divorce, just so happened to be friends with a medium from a place not too far from my village, I think her name was Caroline. We jumped in her car and went to see her friend. I was so happy and relieved; someone believed me, actually really believed. I'm not sure if I told her everything that had happened, but I told her enough to warrant the visit. We both sat down at the table when we got there. Caroline mentioned how much extra weight I was carrying, and handed me a piece of paper.

She said that she had been talking to the guy who was always at me, she said that he told her I had found out his name. She then said, "Just so you believe me, open the piece of paper." I opened it and on it was the name 'Brendan'. She asked 'What's his name?' and said I said 'Brendan.' She took out a crystal that was swinging on a chain, said whatever needed to be said and sent them on to wherever it was they needed to go. Apparently on his way out, he told her that he would be back from time to time. I never liked that.

Altogether she said that there were nine of these energies in my house, mainly in my room. My negative mindset fuelling them, drawing them to me, there was an open doorway in my room and she would have to close it. She told me that I was extra sensitive to these things, that I would naturally draw energies to me, that's what she liked to call them. And she then told me that she could teach me how to strengthen this, and develop it further. I straight out asked "Will I see a person? If I have to go downstairs in the middle of the night will I see a man standing there?" She said "Yes that can happen," and I just said "No. I don't want to see that or anything else ever again, I just want it to be over." And she respected that. I never saw her again after that night. My auntie brought me home, we ripped down the posters on my bedroom walls, lit some sage and could not believe the change in the atmosphere. It was warm for the first time in years, it was so nice. I've never felt anything in that house since, although one of my sisters has said she often sees an old man peeking into the kitchen.

I never figured out if the wailing noise I heard was connected to the stuff that happened in my house. I don't know if it was all down to the same entity or if it was just down to me being hyper-sensitive to that world and throughout that time attracted different things like the medium said...., something your readers can hopefully figure out for me........'

~ ~ ~

Reverend Ted Pike, who runs a national prayer network in the States, spoke publicly to his followers in the aftermath of a particularly gruelling number of years, which culminated in personal tragedy. "It is with great reluctance that I reveal the bizarre circumstances that led to my wife's death." He was reluctant, he said, because, by revealing the circumstances, " I will almost certainly destroy my credibility with readers whose beliefs excludes the Supernatural."

It seems that it all began many years ago, and it began with him. In 1971, in his mid twenties, after many years of Bible Study and comparative interpretations of the Bible, he decided to write a very controversial religious book, which would heavily critisize one particular religious group. Seeking solitude in which to write, he went off to a cabin in the Mountains, a perfect location from which to compose his book. However, something very strange happened. It began suddenly, very soon after arriving there. "I became very weak; so weak that I couldn't walk more than a few feet without needing to lay down. I began to experience visitations of what were very tangible presences in the night, which would temporarily paralyse me while overwhelming me with the sensations of evil. This continued for more than a decade and I could only do light work for less than twenty minutes. If I persisted I would become so exhausted I would become immobilized for days at a time.

This went on for years. Then he met his beautiful young wife, an artist. "After marrying, my wife, who used to walk ten miles a day and play the piano for hours a day, suddenly became extremely weak. She experienced inexplicable exhaustion, just like mine. We tried to go on honeymoon, but we went barely a few kilometres before she became so sick and nauseous that she had to lie down beside the roadside."

Of course, one could suggest that this had to be a

form of emotional contagion, and she fell under the impression of her new husband, her body mirroring his as he sunk into exhaustion. However, if she was somehow subconsciously copying him, she was even sharing his nightmares. "Once, while sleeping, I dreamt that an evil man was coming toward me, his hands about to strangle me. We awoke simultaneously. She said she'd had a nightmare, that an evil man was coming toward her neck, his hands out to strangle her."

Not long after marrying, they had gone out for a walk one late summer evening, and were walking in a large rock quarry. Suddenly, his wife exclaimed that she could see streaking, flashing lights across the Sky. She said there was an enormous black silhouette of a man's torso and head in the heavens. As we left to go home, she said lights were appearing among the trees. In the years following, there were thousands of supernatural intrusions. Some will certainly say that what my wife experienced were hallucinations after she had brain surgery to remove a tumour. But she was not alone. I experienced it.

After our walk at the Quarry, this is only a small example of what we both experienced; presences, faces; the house was filled with presences. Sickening odours. Water dripped from dry ceilings. She saw an eye staring at her from inside the sink hole. She saw creatures like worms swarming around in the darkness. We heard scurrying. We heard banging. I saw tiny red lights in the house, in the trees. There were knocks on our doors but no one there. Human-like forms come in and out of our house. Our cats would flee from them. Garbled messages were left on our phone.

They told her they were going to kill her and she didn't have a chance; they were too many. The cats would flee. She would hear music from no known source, which I would also sometimes hear. Objects would disappear and then reappear a few hours later in a place we couldn't have missed. A stapled page, page 5, disappeared. A few hours later it had rejoined the stapled pages. A manuscript was discovered thrown into a stove and burnt.

She once said she saw an airliner descending toward

the airport turn into a serpentine dragon. She saw UFOs hovering over the landscape. Once, as we were taking a walk in the night, she saw glowing eyes staring at her out of the woods. Then, coming directly over the trees we both saw a bright white light which turned a glowing red. She would frequently see human figures outside our house, including a man in a baseball cap, standing on the top of a fir tree. There would be knocks at the door; but no-one there. Often I would see tiny, intense red lights in the trees and fields. Once, she pointed out to what were large grass-green squares imposed like lattice on the forest. One night she was lifted and thrown back and forth across a room. Another time she was thrown head first down a cliff. Somehow, she survived.

A regular runner, at the local track, she asked a tall, handsome, young runner what he thought she should do about her constant knee pain. He told her to run to the limit but back off if the pain got too great. As he walked away, she saw him de-materialize through a fence. She continued to run. She injured her knees, blew them out, and could never run again. In 2011, his wife got in her car alone in the middle of the night, drove to Marquam   Bridge, and jumped into Willamette River. 'Did she commit suicide? No,' says her husband. 'Satan murdered her, throwing her off the bridge.'

His parents, he says, though they professed a belief in the supernatural, were very reluctant to accept that there were these "intrusions" taking place. The Reverend says, "People don't want to accept these; they need comfort in their lives. They can accept such things may exist, but they do not want to accept they are visibly in our lives." For those who will dismiss his account as gross exaggeration and fantasy, he took the precaution of taking statements after her bizarre death, from an array of those who knew her. He says that he shared her experiences at the time they were happening, with a close group of family members and friends. So, they knew it was happening, but would they corroborate it? There were many who did.

Mary Ann Pike, his niece said; "I heard her upstairs screaming. One thing that seemed to happen; she had these major attacks when he was writing or publicly speaking out......It was always in correlation to this, always when he was fighting religious laws and such."

Family friend, Peggy said; "It seemed like these forces were manipulating her thoughts. She babbled incoherently expressing concern for family. It was not 'her.' I didn't know if they were going to take her for good. I just remember they were horrifying experiences....."

~ ~ ~

In 1651, Parliamentarian and General, Oliver Cromwell was leading his army in what was to be the most brutal military victory ever to have taken place in the British Isles. Cromwell was leading the Roundheads against King Charles II and his army of Cavaliers and the Scots, who had taken side with the King. Cromwell's Army entered Scotland to embark on their bloody battle against the Scots, from which they emerged victorious. He then led the final great battle of the English Civil War of September 1651.

On September 3rd, they were camped up and positioned in a place called Pirie Wood, in the County of Worcester, with a full battalion of artillery, awaiting their battle. Early that morning, Cromwell strode into the tent of his lieutenant, Colonel Thomas Lindsay and woke him up in a manner of urgency. He told his Colonel to hurry and dress, telling him, "I need your protection. I must meet with someone in the woods and you must witness something."

His Colonel dressed quickly and went with the General, riding off on their horses toward the thick forest, and going deep inside it. As they reached a stopping point, the Colonel would later say that he became seized with horror and trembling, after seeing "something strange in the aspect of the General." He meant, that there was something in the General's face that caused him to feel a sudden instinct of absolute terror.

"I have never felt, in all my battles, so overcome that I couldn't continue. And yet I was suddenly conscious of an unnatural, indescribable feeling." He was rooted to the spot. The General told him to watch closely and listen and to bear witness to what was to happen, then dismounted and walked a short distance toward some thick trees. The Colonel assumed that they would be meeting with Spies; he couldn't have been more wrong. The mist that had seemed to shroud them as they had ridden through the forest, suddenly cleared and an unusual black-robbed figure with a cowl over his head now stood there. The Colonel later described him as an elderly man with a grey beard and a grave face. The figure unrolled a piece of parchment and handed it to the General.

The Lieutenant said that on reading what was on the parchment, the General's face "darkened with fury. He shouted angrily at the robed figure; "You have broken your word. Our agreement was for 125 years and yet you offer me 7!" The General asks for double. "If you don't take it, there will be others who will," replied the shrouded figure. The General accepted, turned away, and walked back to where the Colonel had been observing the interaction. The old man had vanished, as though instantaneously.

The General' s mood however, had lifted from anger to joy. "His mood now was one of barely suppressed delight, as he burst out with: "We have the Battle won!!" And, indeed, they did win. The Colonel said that they won due to terrible and unexpected errors made by the enemy soldiers. So perturbed by the encounter in the woods however, the Colonel deserted the Battle and went AWOL. He fled the country and asked for sanctuary in a foreign land. "I could take no more of such things," he said.

Before he left, he told the Clergy; "The King's forces are

defeated, and Cromwell will die this day in seven years, for he has sold himself to the devil, who will not fail to claim him."

Perhaps it was just coincidence, but the General did indeed die 7 years to the day of that strange meeting in the forest, on February 3rd, 1658. Others say he died of Malaria and that was all; however, on the night of his death, 7 years to the day of his pact with the robed figure in the woods, one of the wildest storms to ever hit England came, causing devastation in its path, sinking ships, destroying homes, and bringing down hundreds of trees. It was said that the storm was caused by the Devil coming to collect the General and drag him to Hell.

Chapter 5: Baffling Mysteries

An Australian politician and Justice of the Peace went to his grave without ever getting an answer to the mysterious death of his son. His son had been found on their farm property in Tellbang, Queensland, dead in a field, in 1971. The politician, Lindsay Hartwig, was a Member of Queensland Legislative Assembly and a Judge. He was a well-educated and very rational man, not accustomed certainly to any outlandish speculation or claims; however, something would happen to him too that would make him reconsider everything he thought he knew.

On June 11th 1971, his 19-year-old son Graham had gone out into the fields to fix fences with one of the farm workers. He was later found dead, but his cause of death was never determined. His files too have been sealed. Earlier that day, the politician had been out on his property and had stumbled across a ring of dead grass, approximately six meters in diameter. Where it was found, bordered an area of heavily forested shrub. It appeared to look like the grass had been burned somehow, although the grass inside of the perfect cylinder shaped burn was healthy. His son had then apparently vanished later that day, while he was out on the extensive property helping the farm worker, at a distance of about two kilometers from the farm house. When he was found dead, he had a strange mark on his face, but it was said that the Doctor in attendance would not let his Father see it up-close. His son's body was lying just 150 meters from the circle of burnt ground that his father had stumbled across earlier, before his son had disappeared.

Two years later, the father was out alone in his truck. When he described what happened next, he said: "Now, I'm sane; and, I'm a bushman. I was the greatest disbeliever in flying objects; yet, there in the sky hung two pale green objects, like gemstones. They were oval. This is something I have never been able to answer, and it takes me back to my son's death." He asks rhetorically and alluding to the idea that these spheres were from a dimension or place other than our world, where other 'beings' lived; "Did he meet up with these people?"

Bill Chalker, for *Australian Physical Trace Cases* recorded that a few months after the son's death, there was still a 6 -meter-wide ring next to the heavily forested shrub on the politician's property. He said it was burnt grass, which may or may not have been of fungal properties, and that it was a perfect circle. He also verified that the son had been found about 150m away from the circle. He added that it was reported there was a strange mark on his face, but an autopsy was unable to reveal a cause of death.

The UFOIC, (The UFO Investigation Centre for Australia) also noted that same year, a small child in New South Wales had reported a "boat" with lights over the roof of their home, at 3 am., which hovered then disappeared really fast. The next morning the child's father discovered a dark patch in the front lawn. A Dr Geoff Stevens later examined the ground and found "grey powder." The powder has never been identified as any known natural phenomenon....

Fifteen minutes by car from Tellebang brings you to Mulgildie. It is here that local people from successive generations claim that the Bunyip lurk. The bunyip are said to lurk in swamps, creeks, riverbeds, and waterholes. Exactly what the bunyip is however, has never been entirely established. The word 'bunyip' is translated from the Aboriginal dialect as meaning "devil,' or "evil spirit." From as far back as 19th century accounts of this 'being,' descriptions include those of a strange creature with a dog-like face. It was said to be "11 paces long" and "4 paces in breadth." The legend of the bunyip has lived long in Australian history. With Aboriginal Elders and generations of farmers having told tales about the eerie sensation of hearing the sound of bubbling water, and of their cattle then mysteriously disappearing. Residents in this small township of Mulgildie say they have a waterhole where the bunyip live. 'The Bunyip Hole' is a still pool covered in green slime, and it is known to gurgle. The belief is that this hole is connected to an underground waterway network. Local woman Joan Farrell moved to the area in 1970's and she told reporters, "You don't go there, especially in the dark, and you don't swim in it, because you can get dragged down never to be seen again."

The problem is no-one really knows what one looks like exactly; Part crocodile, part-dinosaur, with a dog-like head, or more like a bird's head. Dark fur, facial horns and a bulky physique. The size of a cow. An aggressive animal with supernatural powers. It is said to lurk in billabongs and rivers awaiting its next meal and according to Aboriginal legend, that meal is sometimes human. It warns its victims of their imminent doom with a terrifying howl. Is this just superstition?735 googled The Sydney Morning Herald on January 4th 1947, wrote of the curious case of the "Wailing at the Waterhole."

Staff writer Bill Beatty said,

"Various theories and conjectures can be offered, but not substantiated, regarding the terrifying screams that come from the Watering Hole over so many years." The Waterhole lies on the way to Isisford, in Central-Western Queensland. He continues; "The records of this uncanny phenomenon are many. It is said that the noises were first heard more than 8 decades ago. It was said by bushmen to be the bunyip. Inevitably, controversy began as to whether there was such a creature, and yet even it was never credited with emitting such blood-curdling screams as those that came from the Watering Hole."

"The many stories are consistent and they always feature a series of terrifying, fiendish yells and screams, that arise suddenly and then die away mysteriously into silence. On record is the account from more than 50 years ago when two shearers, on their way to a station, had camped up by this water-hole on a warm summer evening. The hole was well supplied with water, and after leaving their horses to graze, the two men made tea over their fire, ate dinner, and yarned for a few hours. The fire had nearly died down, and the men yawning, when suddenly there came a soft, distant wailing that grew rapidly nearer and louder.

To the astonishment of the two men, the cries appeared to be in different keys; devilish, unearthly shrieking, such as no human voices have ever uttered. The screaming was now ringing in the men's ears at a deafening pitch, and it was coming from the waterhole. They thought their ear-drums would surely burst, yet they were too terrified to move.

Then, to their fervent relief, the shrieking diminished in volume until it was merely a weird wailing. Moments later, it ceased completely, and all was a deathly silence. Throughout it all, not a ripple came across the surface of the water from which the noises had come.

The men quickly caught their horses and rode off. When the men told their story later at the shearing station, it was received with derision by some, but others there told of it being a notorious spot. They told of instances where cattle had arrived there exhausted, but had stampeded as the sun went down.

The Newspaper continues with another story about a new farmhand who had just been employed at a nearby Station. He had brought his wife with him and they had settled to live in a hut he built by himself near the Watering Hole. She had lived in the outback all her life, and was used to the harsh living and the isolation when her husband was away working long days and nights on the Station. However, they had only been living there a few days when he came home late one night and found his wife in a state of hysteria and near-collapse. She could describe nothing she had seen but had heard the most awful shrieking noises, which seemed to have come from the Watering Hole. Her husband said that it must have been some nocturnal birds. Unfortunately, he was away for two nights soon after this, and on his return he was confronted by the terrible sight of his wife almost having lost her mind. She told him that she had heard the most horrifying screaming and wailing coming from the water. Fearing for her very sanity, her husband took her away from there that very night and they never returned.

On hearing of this incident, at the Station where he worked, a few of the men decided to go down to the Watering Hole and camp out for the night to brave the unknown. They were careful to ensure that they could not be made victims of a practical joke, by placing scouts at posts around them, to ensure no-one crept around down there and spooked them.

They sat around the roaring fire swopping stories and smoking until after midnight, when they settled into their blankets. It started as a soft low wail. By the time they had got to their feet it had reached screaming pitch, of a sound each of them knew was not uttered by bird, beast, or human. They fled as fast as they could and none would ever return there again....

~ ~ ~

It was April 18th 1943, amid World War Two, when four young boys, out hunting for birds nests in the Hagley Woods in the County of Worcestershire, England, came across something they could never have anticipated. Passing a Wych-Hazel tree, they noticed its large hollow trunk and they couldn't resist investigating it. The smallest of the four boys ventured inside the tree trunk and to his absolute horror, he found a human skull. Jumping out of the tree in terror, he screamed and told the other boys what was inside, and the group of boys fled in fear and shock, running back home as fast as they could, and although they had sworn not to tell a soul about the grisly discovery; the youngest of the boys, so traumatised by the discovery of the skull, which still had patches of hair attached to it, broke down and told his father what he had seen in the tree in the woods.

His father summoned the local constabulary straight away, who descended on the Woods to retrieve the skull and search the scene. Along with the skull was the gruesome remnant of hair still attached to it and tiny bones scattered, along with tatters of clothing the victim had presumably been wearing. The local pathologist at the time, Dr. James Webster determined that on investigation of the bones and the skull, the victim had been a female aged between 30-40 years of age. Chillingly, it appeared that he had also determined she had been placed inside the hollow tree trunk "while still warm," at least one and a half years earlier.

This ruling meant that she had either just been killed when she had been placed inside the tree, with her limbs still flexible enough to position her inside of it, or, she had been forced into the tree alive. Also found with the skull, had been remnants of a piece of taffeta, which had been pushed into her mouth, while she was still alive. All dentists in the area were contacted to see if they could match the pattern of the teeth still attached to the skull; but none could. The cause of the woman' s death was ruled as asphyxiation, caused by the taffeta being pushed inside her mouth. The police however, could find no correlation with any women on their missing person's lists.

Weeks passed by, turning into months, then suddenly graffiti appeared which said; "Who put Bella down the Witch Elm?" The message, cryptic in its question, implied of course that someone clearly knew more about this than the police did, but they weren't sharing it, other than to leave this enigmatic message. The person, who left this graffiti, has never been identified, nor either has the answer to the graffiti's question.

During a BBC Radio retrospective investigation looking back at the case, the journalist was contacted by a woman who had known a lady called Una Mossap, who had been married to a man called Jack. Jack was employed at the time of the incident, at the local munitions factory, purportedly doing manual work and yet he was usually seen in rather dapper clothing, despite the war shortages. He was also alleged to have purchased a Royal Air Force uniform, and villagers said he would often be seen wearing it, despite not actually being in the Royal Air Force at all. He often came into the village to stop off at his grandmother's and to have a drink in the Pub, usually accompanied by another man who was believed to have been from Holland.

Twelve years after 'Bella' had been found dead in the tree; this man's wife had gone to the police and given them a written statement, which said that her husband had confessed to both her and his grandmother, that he had put 'Bella' in the tree. He said the three of them, he, the Dutchman and 'Bella' had been having a drink and that Bella had become "awkward", perhaps meaning that he was saying she had got drunk. In an effort to "cool her down" he said he and the Dutchman had apparently shoved her inside the tree and left her there to calm down and sober up. He didn't say he had out-right killed her; more that her death had occurred as a result of them leaving her there in the tree trunk. He would go on to tell his wife that he was being haunted nightly by the grisly vision of her staring at him, stuck in the tree and dead; her eyes were fixed wide open and staring at him. He died at the age of 29 in an asylum for the insane, even before her body had been found in the tree.

Interestingly, Professor Norma Fenton who applies mathematical and statistical probability to criminal evidence, stated that the likelihood, based on evidence, that Jack had killed 'Bella' was actually only 31%. That's not to say he didn't kill her or commit manslaughter, but rather that the available evidence could only statistically say it was 31% likely. The investigation into the woman's death was to take many twists and turns over the years; with some saying she had been a prostitute from a City outside of the area, others pointing to the Gypsy community as having had an internal fight and her death resulting, while there was also the intriguing possibility that she had been a Spy. A woman called Anna contacted the police to tell them of a Spy ring in operation that involved 'Bella.' She claimed that Bella was in fact a dance-hall singer who was also an undercover Spy for the Nazi's.

In the '60's, researcher Donald McCormick said Bella was both a Spy and an occultist, whose name was "Clarabelle", and who had been recruited by the Nazi's to infiltrate the munitions factories nearby. Of course, none of this could be absolutely corroborated, but it did capture the public imagination when the story was trickled out by the Newspapers, in an era when the James Bond novels begun being published. Mysteriously, her remains also disappeared, and no-one seems to know where they are nor her final resting place.

Curiously, a few months after the skull and remains had been found, a leading anthropologist by the name of Professor Margaret Murray added more mystery to the case by citing the possibility that it could have been a disturbing occult ritual ceremony called "The Hand of Glory," and theorising that the scattered finger bones that were found with the skull indicated that a ritualistic murder had taken place. The Professor's position was that Bella had been summarily executed in this ceremony and her hand removed and taken to be used as a "Hand of Glory."

The Professor had already written books on the subjects of the Occult and Witchcraft across Europe, and it was her belief that there was a secret cabal of Witches who had infiltrated the highest levels of English aristocracy and political power. Less than an hour's drive away, two years after "Bella" or "Clarabelle's death there had incidentally been the "witchcraft killing" of farmer Charles Walton, who had been found lying in a field, a pitchfork embedded into him, pinning him to the ground, and a cross carved into his chest.

As for the "Hand of Glory," it is said to be the left hand that is taken; the hand of the 'Left Path.' In the case of executed prisoners, where the taking of a "Hand of Glory" was said to be more common, this would be the hand deemed to have committed the offence, literally the hand that had done the evil deed. The hand would be removed from the executed prisoner, taken away, and pickled or dried out. Often more was taken from the dead person too; the fat of the corpse would be used to create the candle wax, and the candle, when created, would be placed into the stiff dead hand. The belief was that this "Hand of Glory" now held great but evil power, and that the Hand holding the lit candle could stop anyone in their paces. It was believed it would 'freeze' a person. It would prevent a person from moving, from leaving, when confronted by it.

The hand of a hanged prisoner was most sought after, as it was believed that the more evil the person's crime, the greater the power of their hand would be for magical purposes. In olden times, possession of a "Hand of Glory" was much sought after by thieves, in the belief that it aided them when house-breaking and robbing, by freezing and entrancing the occupants of the houses they robbed from. A real "Hand of Glory" is actually on display at the Whitby Museum, in Yorkshire, England.

Whether or not Bella's hand was taken for this purpose, or not; and whether she was a dance-hall singer but really a Nazi Spy, has never, completely been established, which perhaps makes it all the more intriguing. Or, perhaps it was in fact, the result or the man who impersonated a Royal Air force service man, who hadn't meant to kill her, just shut her up, but who as a result of his actions had been driven insane by her spirit returning to haunt him, sending him to the lunatic asylum where he died at a remarkably young age......

~ ~ ~

Inside a bedroom, in a Castle built by hand, in the middle of a National Forest, hung a portrait. It was a self-portrait of the owner of the Castle, and the disturbing image depicted him from the neck up, and his mouth gagged. In his forehead, blood was pouring from a series of bullet wounds. Sometime later, he would say, "I deserved all of this."

So was the true story of the man who had left the world behind and taken his younger lover to live in the woods, away from civilization and surrounded only by the barren winter trees and a library of books. Among the books were tomes on kabbalah, spirituality, the occult, and "devil-worship."

It was the "devil-worship" which would attract the most attention later, when exactly as his self-portrait depicted, he was found gagged and shot to death, with blood pouring from the bullet wounds in his forehead. The question is of course, how could he have known he would die in such an identical manner? It's a tale replete with eccentricity, violence, drugs, sex, allegations of the conjuring of a demon, death, and hauntings. Their "Castle," it seems, was a private bacchanalia, with the occasional invited guest, before its catastrophic ending came about.

The owner and builder of this "Castle" was 56 year old Professor Lee Charles Scudder. He had resigned from his position as Associate Professor at Loyola University in Chicago. He had gained his PhD at the University and had held a Research post at the University's Institute for Mind, Drugs, and Behaviour, until his resignation in 1977. He had at one time been married and his marriage had produced two children, who by the time he built his Castle, had reached adulthood. When he moved out of the City to a densely wooded part of the Chattooga National Forest, near Summerville, Georgia, the closest community to the land he purchased was Trion, and the nearest road from his land was more than two miles away. He took with him 37 year old Joseph Odom and together, as lovers, they constructed by hand their new home, taking inspiration from the Castles of the medieval age.

According to Sheriff McConnell, who later talked to the Chicago Tribune, "There were skulls scattered throughout the house." Later, it would be said the inside of the home was "Like the scene from a horror movie." The Newspaper described it as "Adorned with skulls, satanic altars, and bizarre sexual instruments." It had a pink gargoyle on its roof and a stained glass window depicting Baphomet, and a dog named 'Beelzebub.'

"The man's life is a mystery," the Sheriff said, of the Professor. However, he added, "His life for the last

few years pointed to "devil worship." At the time that
the Sheriff was commenting, arrest warrants had
been issued for two Georgia men from the nearest
community who had been at the Professor's home,
and they were now wanted for robbery and murder.
It was 1982, and the Professor and his lover had
been killed in their Castle. The Professor's last words
had been. "I deserved this all," after his lover had
been killed and he knew he was next, and eerily, he
was killed just as his self-portrait showed.

The Sheriff who had been giving statements said that
on discovery of the Professor's body by a friend who
had arrived at the residence to give some important
news, he had since been trying to "piece together"
the life the Professor had been leading, but that he
had only so far "reconstructed pieces." Much
emphasis was given to the homosexual relationship
between the Professor and his younger lover, with the
Sheriff saying the younger man was the older man's
"servant, lackey; his boy." The Newspapers were
quick to pick up on the most lurid aspects of the case,
such as the "pink pleasure room" in which it was

alleged they engaged in their bacchanalia with each other, and the suggestion was, with other male visitors too, including one of the boys who later shot them both to death. Around the Castle were bizarre images of "bestiality and other paraphernalia involving sexual activity and devil worship."

The Sheriff and the locals were very much of the opinion that the Castle was a place for the demonic, given perhaps more because the area itself was thoroughly considered part of the 'bible-belt' at the time. Of course, arriving at the Castle to find the slaughter, they would have seen the stained glass window depicting Baphomet, the horned goat, the altar inside, and the bookshelf of 'satanic books;' although there were other books there too, on spirituality, and religion. The scattered skulls were gathered up and taken to the F.B.I.'s crime Lab and the bodies of course, examined and taken away. They had been lying there for five days.

On the night of the killings, it seems that according to the testimonies of those who participated and those who witnessed, the younger of the men was shot with a rifle while in the kitchen, after Kenneth Brock, Tony West, his cousin and his cousin's girlfriend had all arrived on casual invite, to have some wine with the couple at their Castle. It also transpired that one of the men, Kenneth, had allegedly been there on several occasions prior to this night, and engaged in forms of sexual activity in the "pleasure room" with the couple.

The night of the killings, the group had arrived en-masse. Some of them, on the way there, took a combination of "drugs" together called 'Toot-a-loo;' an unappetizing combination of alcohol, glue, and paint-thinner, to get high. Brook was alleged to have said that he had been to the castle on multiple occasions and had intimate interaction with the two men who lived there, while sharing LSD.

It appeared most likely that the motive for the slaughter was robbery, although the police and authorities of the day, as well as the Newspapers, were most interested in the skulls, gargoyles and books on the devil. The killers themselves are said to have been motivated more by the mistaken belief that this couple had a lot of money. The Castle was not opulent, and certainly, having been built in a very rudimentary manner by the couple who had no training in house construction, it was not a luxurious palace. It was in fact very basic, so much so that when one of the killers pulled the gag out of the Professor's mouth to ask him where the soldering iron was so that he could plug it in to torture him, the Professor answered that there was no electricity supply, as well as no running water and no indoor bathroom.

The strangest thing perhaps was that the Professor's two dogs, both huge English mastiffs and described as "the size of Shetland ponies" by the attending Sheriff, did not stir at all during the slaughter. A trail of bloody footprints had led the Sheriffs to the body of the Professor, leading from the body of his lover. Detective Tony Gilleland said that the suspects had fired shots at the younger man as he was in the kitchen, and that he had then crawled from the kitchen to the living room where the Professor was being gagged and tied up with strips of a bedsheet. A rope was around his neck. The gag was removed to ask the Professor where his iron was so they could torture him. At this point, he tried to walk toward his younger lover, who now lay dead in front of him, only to be told to sit back down; but it was said by the witnesses there, Joe Wells and Teresa Hudgins, that he refused to sit down, refused to stop walking, and said aloud; "I deserve all of this."

He was then shot five times in the head, just as his self-portrait had depicted. Close-by lay his dead dogs, who had been shot before him, without them stirring or attacking, despite the gunshots that killed Odom. "That's what Dr Scudder looked like when we found him," said Detective Gilliland at the scene, pointing at the self-portrait, but the painting was not in the room in which the killings took place, and it was believed that the killer had never been inside the room in which it hung. Also strange was that although Joe Wells and Teresa say they left when things turned began to turn nasty, when they got to their car outside of the "castle," they both said the car wouldn't start. They returned back inside, unable to leave and forced to watch as the two men were slaughtered. This could have been said for the purposes of creating an alibi; to show that they did not partake in the killings or any planning of them, however, it wasn't seen that way in Court and in fact, perhaps the truth of it could be backed up more by what's said to have happened there ever since the killings.

Many curious people have visited the ruins of the castle in the middle of the forest, and say they have had some very uncomfortable and unnerving experiences while there, the least of which includes having car trouble, and that they have struggled to explain their experiences as anything other than supernatural. Sometime after the murders, the place was vandalised and burnt, but the curious have sometimes wished they had not gone to see the remains there at all.

The two killers were long gone by the time one of the Professor's friends arrived five days later, and they had killed again while fleeing the county, killing a driver and stealing his car, but they were easily apprehended after pawning off the measly proceeds of their crime- which was very little, just a few nickels and some small items from the home. The confession given by West to Chattooga County Detectives was; *"All I can say is they were devils and I killed them, that's how I feel about it."*

This of course, could have simply been an expression, a phrase, and not literal in its meaning. Mark Fulk, a medium who lives only minutes from the site and who grew up around the time of the killings, had knowledge of a 'satanic' group in the area, who he had loosely associated with, he says, until he realised the true darkness they were involved in. He says the group would go there to conduct rituals with the Professor and Odom. The exact nature of the interactions that took place between visitors to the isolated home in the woods and their hosts is shrouded in mystery, speculation, and accusation, with viewpoints hotly debated, and vast disagreements. Over the years since, some people have left messages in forums saying that they merely held homosexual parties and that on the night of the murders, the two hosts had not even drunk any alcohol, (they had no alcohol in the autopsy results) while others have alleged, unsubstantiated other than self-claimed eye-witnesses, there were cages in the grounds, for humans.

There was the added mystery of the vials of concentrate LSD found in the home, and the defence's legal position when representing the murderers was that the hosts would routinely drug their visitors with the LSD. This of course, has not been proven, or at least, the victims haven't come forward if it did happen, or, it has not been made public, if they have. Defenders of the Professor say that he simply wanted privacy and a quiet life and that was why he went to live in the National Park. Certainly there was nothing in his professional life that pointed to any kind of occultic behaviour.

Of course, a tantalizing link could be made between the Professor's research studies and his subsequent new life in the country and the claims of strange things there; one of his research studies involved, for example, "Methamphetamine sulfate administered in acute and chronic experiments, at constant or increasing doses, to rodents" in August 1971, with the behavioral effects described as "Aggression, sexual, sleeping behaviors quantitated." His research experiments and studies seemed to revolve around rodents, not humans of course, as far as is known. Certainly though, the investigators did find vials filled with pure *LSD*-25. The defence team for the killers offered the idea that the killers had been drugged by this LSD and as a result were temporarily "insane" at the time of the shootings; but the wine that had been served that night did not have traces of LSD in it. Rumors, unsubstantiated, still float around the area however, that this was a site where victims were drugged, bound, and psychologically and even physically tortured.

A. Welch says: "I was there days after the murders with a relative on the law enforcement team. I was 13. In the "Chicken Coop," there were hundreds of photos, some looking as if they were in a stupor, drunk or drugged. Some looked a bit scared, all alone, and the pictures looked - I dunno - more like a photo record than sexy. The pictures were all similar. They looked more like something you would see in sort of a concentration camp.."

Another local person writes: "I was part of a group that

partied up there - we were occultists at that time. He was involved with mind control and linked to the CIA and MKUltra project. They found pure LSD highly purified like the CIA had. I always felt - from looking at those photos - that they were preying somehow." Another local says; "I have Super 8 film, showing odd ritualistic ceremonies."

Could any of this be true? Other counter- responses come from one local lady who says; "To all those who go there to mock or get a thrill, be careful what you do there. Because if I'm wrong and those two really were friends of Satan then you'll eventually meet him there. I would suggest steering clear and closing your mouths. A demon is looking for somebody to feed its evil energy. Don't be stupid and become prey. Stay out of the woods."

Former D.A. Amy Petulla, who researched the case herself, said "It was occasionally whispered that he had invoked a Demon." The sign at the beginning of their property, she says, which read, "Beware of the Thing", led some locals to fear this was referring to something invoked. She adds that the Professor had claimed to have summoned a Demon to protect them there.

A former anonymous Satanist says; "I've been there several times. During the day, it has a calming, serene feeling. After dark it's the complete opposite. He was involved with the CIA and MKULTRA. I used to be into Satanism and all that jazz, so I know respecting that place is imperative. I don't practice anymore, but dark forces are in that place. Spray painting, graffiti etc isn't recommended..."☐

Others believe this is just all just gossip and rumor and exaggeration."His research was brilliant, but it was in areas not considered especially "glamorous; He wasn't part of any mind control experimentation!"

At the conspiratorsnest blogspot, several years ago the author there pointes out;"This gained very little media attention, but it Fits into a small corner of the history of MK Ultra. His past and the evidence at the crime scene, place him into the early days of the project. At the University, he helped play a part by working to recreate LSD- 25, which the C.I.A. had bought. In Liverpool John Moore's University is a series of papers and research for a project called; "Challenge to the Paradigm," which was to be published as a book. He was a contributor and was to contribute titles of his research papers including 'Mindless meaning; meaningless mind.' His work with the mind and psycho-reactive drugs, would have been of serious interest to the C.I.A."

This blogger says "his academic life has been virtually ignored and are yet so very intriguing; the C.I.A. connection stunning." He points out the results of one of the research projects he undertook with LSD, cited by the Professors as, "Certain neurological and behavioural aberrations due to methamphetamine were noted."

A contributor to this forum also makes makes a very interesting point, having read the article about the Professor. "What's funny is that this area (Georgia) is notorious for methamphetamine addicts and methamphetamine cooks: Who brought the technique into this area? And who studied the affects of overloading with methamphetamine? -The Professor! ...He seems like a nice guy, from reading his own article in *Mother Earth Journal*, (one in which the Professor describes in length his move to the backwoods, to be with nature and away from the City) but hmmm....could he have been involved in the release of this epidemic in our region as part of the extended study, of those behind MK Ultra?"

Surely, this is taking things too far!, and it really can't

be said that the Professor did "release" LSD or Methamphetamine into the population at all, (although the quantity of LSD he had, would have dosed up the entire State, it was so concentrate.) Again, this is all just one person's thoughts and again, completely uncorroborated, but it's an interesting line of thought none the less, despite being wholly without evidence.

An attempt to recreate the drug domestically? A drug allegedly first used by Nazis to keep their soldiers awake for days? -Most likely completely fantasy, as with the 'summoned demon' and the allegations of worshipping the devil and drugging of local men, but still, the answer as to why the Doctor painted himself dying in the exact way in which he did later die; with something around his neck, gagged and shot five times in the forehead, and his last words, "I deserve all of this," remains elusive and unexplained still….it's the riddle of the last words uttered by the Professor; "I deserve all of this," and the foreboding self-portrait which seemed to predict his death and the exact manner in which he would die, which is most mysterious in all of this.

Interestingly, Gregory Myers, of Missouri Paranormal Group, writes a strange tale in which he says he was contacted by an individual who had known the Professor in Chicago, and that after his murder, this individual was now awaiting the arrival of a package which contained artefacts taken from the Castle. The man had approached Gregory Myers to ask him to receive the package. Myers says, "Only a higher power would know why he wanted such artefacts and why he would want a paranormal group to study them for residual energy. I have to ask what potential for evil would these artefacts still have? I was curious at first; would they emit EMF, or anomalies? I talked to the individual who was awaiting their arrival and learnt that the items were still sealed in the box they had been stored in after the murders and had not been touched since. I learnt that "radiating power" could be felt from this sealed box."

"This information led me to realise that they did not need to be handled nor studied. There was other facts too that persuaded me that opening this box would be dangerous. I was convinced the items in the sealed box were potentially some sort of key connecting one's soul to a dark element. Evil can arrive at your doorstep, evil beyond your imagination, and its curiosity that opens that

Pandora's Box and allows it to infest. I truly believe the Professor believed he was on a ritualistic path that could make him a dark equal in an infinite existence. As such, due to the dark aspects involved in this, I recommended to this individual that these items should be left in that box, bound with a cross and dropped in a flowing river, forever sealed."

Is this just overly dramatic, or, did he make the right decision? Stigmatised for their life-style amid a conservative bible-belt back in the early '80's, wild unsubstantiated rumours and gossip about drugged young men and torture, and piles of photographs taken; were the couple just quiet homesteaders, just wishing to live a peaceful and secluded life of freedom, and the Professor just an educated man with an intellectual curiosity about alternative religions and philosophy? Or, not? How did the Professor know that he was going to die in the exact manner in which he had portrayed in his own self-portrait?

That's the real mystery.....

~ ~ ~

In Volume 3. of the 1947 Round Robin Bulletin of Contact and Information from the Borderland

Sciences Research Foundation, comes a strange story sent into them and presented at a Conference for scrutiny. The editors of the bulletin found the man's account to appear to be of veracity, including the photographs he provided to supplement his account. They also add as a word of caution, that any ideas of investigating the area he talks about as "bold adventurers armed with machine guns" might well be "disastrous folly."

Mr E. Johns had contacted them to tell of his experiences, which occured when he moved to the area of the Mendocino Mountain Range in California in 1930 with his mother, to make a homestead there. Once they had purchased the land, they built a very basic home and decided to have some of the forest cut down close to the house in order to sell firewood to raise the funds they needed to finish their home to a higher standard. They hired a lumberjack to chop down some of the trees, and Johns and his mother made the journey to the closest town to sell the firewood. They were away for two days. When they returned, the lumberjack came up to them, told them to keep the bond money he had given them as a 'promise' that he would complete their work for them, and said he would not continue the work nor would he ever come back there. He would not explain to them his reason; he simply told them that under no circumstance would he ever return there.

All was well for the first few nights after he left. Then things began to get very strange. "We could hear noises that did not belong; many horses drinking water though there was no water; I didn't have a water supply, and when I went outside I saw nothing. The door knob would turn of its own accord. I shot through the door and then it quit. There was a phenomenon of bright lights at night over the house, as though there was a streetlamp and as though the place had moved to town. It stayed like that all night but I was never able to find out where they came from.

A couple of weeks later, I was introduced to the little people. At first I thought they were figments of my imagination. I would soon learn better. They were followed by what I now know are Undines and Sylphs.

They would surround me. They would ask me childish questions such as "What is a gun?" I asked them where they live and they showed my all of the secrets they were allowed to. It appeared that the land I had was in the centre of their domain and that it changes into their vibration at times; but that if I were to enter their land I would be unable to return. The secrets are not for the average person to know and so I would rather not tell them. I have been given the power to find all secrets. There is no secret that I cannot find if I wish to and technical things that are far beyond anything science has today; but many of these things should be forgotten I feel, for the people are not ready for such knowledge yet. I have lived with these things now and have been very lucky to escape alive. My luck may not protect everyone who goes into such a world. I tried to get a tree Nymph to come with me, but the 'ruling power' would not allow this to happen. I see now why, but I did not at the time.

In the kitchen window at sundown one day, we saw a pair of eyes staring at us. They were five inches in diameter. They glowed reddish, very bright. When I went outside I saw nothing; they had vanished. When I went back in the house, they reappeared. This game continued for twenty minutes. Then they went away. While they were going away we saw a large shape like three large cones piled one on top the other. This shape went across the meadow. I never found out what that was.

One night, at around 10 p.m. we saw two cars drive down the road to the end, or so we thought. The road they were on was a narrow trail that ends at a Canyon, with no way to turn around. You have to back up all the way. The next morning we followed the car tracks. They ended against a boulder and that was that. Never did learn where they went. I have had hints since then, but I do not care to enlarge upon them. Several "perfect crimes" have been committed here. A man murdered two wives near the Canyon. He was later found dead in his car with the doors shut and windows locked. One empty rifle was in his hands and a loaded rifle beside him. The coroner never did find out what killed him.

Also there is a phenomenon. When you try to walk up the mountain it's like walking through molasses, and when you go down you are pushed down faster than you would wish. Some are bodily thrown as far as twenty feet." After he moved away from the area, he returned on many occasions. "There is an undercurrent of fear in the area that is intangible but noticed in the people who live in the fringes of the area. Ranches have been abandoned. It is useless to fight the spirits. Anyone who attempts to build a home here it seems, usually comes to grief, one way or another, and we have been no exception to the rule; however, we were smart enough to get out while still able."

Say the Editors of the Journal to which the man sent in the story of his experiences which occurred; "The phenomena of the lights and the huge eyes have many parallels. We have no reason to question the correctness of his accounts as far as our information stands. Phenomena of this type do not call for an expedition with guns; for any folly of that sort might well be disastrous...."

~ ~ ~

An Italian reader currently living in Iceland, advised me to take a look into the Icelandic culture and beliefs, as well as the real experiences of people there, with regards to the existence of elementals from other dimensions who seemingly live along side us, and the possible tie-in with people who go missing there in very strange circumstances. Ricky pointed me first to a website called TheElfSchool. At this 'school,' in Reykjavik, there is a teacher called Mr. Magnus Skarphedinsson, who is an anthropologist with more than four decades of experience in researching Elves and other "hidden people." He says he has interviewed more than 800 Icelanders who have met these "hidden people" and had long-term "friendships" with them. He says he has spoken with people who say they have been invited into the "Hidden People's" homes, have eaten their food, and have even slept in their "homes" with them.

He's also been to many other countries across the world, and met many other people who have had the same experiences in their home countries; so the phenomenon it seems is not restricted to Iceland alone. At this school however, (a loose term, as the attendance for those interested in learning about the "hidden people" is a day's event and does not require a full-time attendance) the school offers to enlighten and educate those who attend, by giving them the ability to understand what the "other dimensions" are where the Elves and the Hidden People say that they live. The Hidden People include not just Elves but Trolls, Gnomes, Fairies, Mountain Spirits and other Nature Spirits. The lessons there also include what these creatures look like, and how they feel about humans.

Lára Bjarnadótir, now an elderly widow, once told the Teacher there of an experience she had as a child, back in the 1930's. She was then living on a farm outside of the town of Brjánslaekur, with her nine siblings and parents. In the large field outside of the farmhouse was a big ragged rock, called 'The Dwarf.' Having heard sinister rumors of the reputation of the rock as they were growing up, including accounts of fishermen who said that at night from the sea they would notice a strange glow coming from inside the rock, the children were always very cautious of approaching it, and they tended to try to avoid it altogether.

But at another spot in one of the other farm fields was also another large rock, but this one had never been given a name, and the children had never heard any sinister stories being told about this rock. It was actually larger than the other rock. One summer's day, the little girl, along with her siblings, was playing close to the large rock. The little girl had scaled up it and was standing at the top of it, skipping around on it, when all of a sudden she heard a loud female voice. It sounded very angry, and it seemed to be coming from right beneath where she was standing. "If you do not get down from the rock at once, you will be punished!" This frightened her so much that she jumped in one leap, down from the top of the rock and ran all the way back inside the farmhouse. Later, her siblings said they had seen no-one else near the rock they had been playing on. There had been no grown woman anywhere in the field, and the siblings had been in sight of her. They were too young to have been able to try to impersonate a lady's loud booming voice, and, it had resonated from under her feet, as though inside of the rock itself. The little girl had never felt such fear in all her young life, and she avoided that rock from then on after her strange experience that day.

At another farm in the region of Sléttuhreppur, there is another large rock, named Steinshóll, that again, stands in the middle of a field. The grass must not be cut near the rock, or bad things will happen. A man called Halldór Guðnason grew up on the property, and he told the anthropologist Mr Skarphedinsson, that one New Years' Eve, when he was 12, he was out in the field playing with a group of his friends from nearby farms. That night there were no clouds in the sky and it was a cold night, with snow on the floor from a snowfall a few nights before.

The children's games had drawn them close to the rock. Suddenly, one of the group asked the little boy Halldor why he was standing stock still and staring at the rock as though in a daze. The little boy had suddenly stopped playing and was standing staring at something no one else could see, completely transfixed. What the boy would later explain was that he had been watching a figure who looked like a Priest, and so handsome, dressed in a rich red robe. He said he had watched the Priest come out of his Church (while all the other boys could only still see the large rock there.) He said that the Priest then started to light fireworks, that went shooting up into the sky. Then the Priest went back inside the Church, and the scene faded away.

A few years later, when this little boy's father decided to ignore warnings and cut the long grass that was surrounding the rock, his sheep began to mysteriously disappear. He did it for three years in a row, and each time, some of his sheep were 'taken.' When he decided to stop cutting the grass around the rock, he never had any more sheep disappear.

Chapter 6: The Stalking Continues

Mateo, an ex-Marine contacted me a while ago, to relate some of his strange experiences in the wilderness. He doesn't know what to make of them, despite being a hardened outdoors-man who spends the vast majority of his time out in the natural environment. "I'm very familiar with the outdoors, and the wildlife. I'm a Marine Corps Veteran of Iraq and Afghanistan. I worked in Infantry and Intelligence. Now, my pursuits are living off-grid and exploring National Forests, particularly the Pike National Forest of Colorado, where I started a long stint far from civilization there. I have a list of strange events in these forests; events that I cannot explain and that have frightened me."

Mateo has asked that his exact location be kept confidential, however, he explains; "It was winter, 2005, around 11 pm, at an elevation of 7.904 ft. My friends and I were going night hiking, heading northward until we got to a rest-stop on the west side of the road that had trails going off into the woods. We got out our gear, food, water, a spot light, and began heading west for about 300 metres in about 1 feet of snow, then the terrain started to angle upward at about 45 degrees. The snow got deeper at about 1 ½ feet. At about 900 feet, I started heading up faster, abandoning my friends who were taking their time, talking. I was about 45 feet from the top when I heard a terrifying part-human, part-animal scream. It was like nothing I have ever heard. I was unable to move, motionless with a fear I could not explain nor understand. Part of me found it illogical that a scream would have this effect on my and yet I was petrified standing there, like some survival instinct had kicked in that had made me stand still.

My friends showed up, I think only about 2 minutes later, but asking them if they heard the screams, I learned that they had not. This made me wonder how further off they actually had been and how much time had actually passed. At first they thought I was joking, mostly because I don't get scared easy, and this was the first time they had seen a reaction such as this, like I'd seen a ghost or something. Finally, it became clear to them that I wasn't joking and they got worried and wanted to go back."

On another occasion in 2014, it was approximately 12 pm, at an elevation of 6,636 feet. "This is in a large area of mostly private property, so most people don't go in here. The terrain is low valleys, large rock spires, and shallow forests. We go there to play "hide and seek;" tracking each other at night. It's a lot of fun. I get to use all the training I had in the Infantry and its great workout!"

"When I arrived, I got there first and so I ran into the cliffs and waited for my friend to get there. He was the hunter, and I was to be the hunted. He called to say he'd arrived and I gave him a description of my location. It was very steep and I could see on both sides of the trail, with brush on the slopes. I waited a while and heard nothing."

"We howl at each other in these games; keeps it intense and you know if someone is on your tail. He sounded really far away. As I howled more it sounded like he was getting closer, and then I heard him creeping on the slope. It sounded as though he was trying to go above me, about 150 metres away. Then I heard his howl again but it sounded like he was further off; I thought he was doing it more softly as a tactic, worried that I could hear him creeping closer to me. He was trying to be quiet but I can hear the gravel. He's trying to flank me but he's close, just above me, about 25 metres away, and then he stops. I keep waiting for him to come and chase me – but there's no sound. Then I hear him start to walk, quietly, softly, over me, flanking me. He's so close I know he's there and I'm getting impatient so I say; "I know you're there – come out! I'm waiting."

He howls – but his howl is from very far away! This set a panic in motion because whoever had snuck up on me, only a few feet away, was not him. I stood frozen, drew out my phone and texted him. He replies that he is not standing next to me. He is half a mile away!" "If it was a mountain lion, I was screwed if I ran, but its step-pattern made me confident it was not. I ran down as fast as I could, making loud noises in hopes of sounding intimidating. I did not look behind me. My friend took a while to reach me - he had thought I was on a different ridge altogether and had been over there....I've run into deer, bears; there are clear difference between bipedal and four legged animals. What I'd heard had been a heavy-set person trying to sneak up on me, flanking me into position. What I know for sure is that someone large tried to flank me. I don't fear much but I didn't investigate further.... It could have been a person; but I doubt they would come after hearing all the howling...."

The following year, in the same general area, again being kept confidential, this time on 26th October, 2015, at an elevation of over 9,000 feet. It was dusk, and in a location several miles inside the National Forest. There was a big bright moon that night. He and his friend were an hour into their hike, with him slightly ahead of the friend by about 20 metres. Fog was coming down as they walked. "I'd walked about 30 metres ahead when I stopped to see where he was behind me. I turned around to see his machete out. I asked him why and he told me, eventually."

"I'd never seen him like this before, so spooked that his body was in fight or flight. He confessed that as the gap between us grew large he noticed something off up the hill at the side of the trail. He had his light on and had beamed in its direction. He described what he saw. He said it was the size of a tall skinny person but strong looking, and with some kind of crown of horns around its head. It was moving, clearly flanking him from above and moving quick in a stealth mode. He said he saw it only for a few seconds before trees covered it. He said he had the distinct impression it was trying to cut him off as I carried on walking further away, as though in order to break the prey from the herd and isolate him."

"I can vouch this was his behaviour; it was one of fear and very defensive. He was so shaken; we've come face to face with bears in the middle of the night and he's had resolve. Now, I was working to keep up with him and he kept looking back. He took a while to tell me but he said he got the impression it had malicious intent. I'll be honest. I do not like being stalked, harassed and hunted by unknown factors and yet this seems to be the recurring theme in my experiences. I'm now of the opinion that there are many "unknowns" with unknown intent yet to be discovered."

~ ~ ~

Jake, on trappers forum trapper man, describes what happened to him; 'This is exactly as it happened; no need to enhance this as it's pretty unbelievable as it is. People have said we're lying or just making it up, but well, what purpose is there in that? I admit freely, I was scared and we were very concerned. It was Darlington Valley, Delaware County, on Thanksgiving Day, back in 1992 and it was 3.30 a.m. There was no moon and heavy cloud cover. Our truck pulled over and we got out into the chill night air, gathering our trapping gear, buckets, and set off down the hill, up a thick valley and across a field, with walls of thick vegetation, then started looping back. In daylight you would only be able to see twenty feet. The only way through it is a narrow deer path.

My friend Arnold and I walked along talking as we checked the coon sets. Strangely, the woods seemed deathly quiet; there were no sounds of deer, rabbits, no owls. There wasn't even any wind. It was a sudden very eerie sensation. Suddenly, every hair on the back of my neck stood up. I'd heard stories of "the Darlington Monster" as a kid, from both my Mother and Father. My Father didn't believe a word of it; my Mother always said "There is something evil in the Valley." I decided it was just animals – foxes screaming, or racoons, or an owl.

We had our flashlights out as we were walking. Suddenly, in front of us this 'thing' lets out this sound. I can't say exactly how it sounded as I'd never heard anything ever before sound like this or anything make this sound. It began as a rumble, like distant thunder, and rose up to a howling shriek, like a banshee. It was so loud it reverberated in my chest. I could feel it strike my face. We looked at each other; "What the ....?" We drew our guns out so fast. Then just as disturbing, there was now no sound, so whatever had made that noise had to be right in front of us just beyond our flashlights. A million thoughts were running through my head. Arnold suggested backing up slowly; I favored the tree and waiting up there until light. He started moving, I went too; I sure wasn't staying there on my own, but we went so slow you'd have thought we were going through a field of mines. Finally, in the pitch dark, we made it out of there.

We've talked about this experience many times since then. We know what we heard; there's over 50 years experience in the woods between us, from swamps to mountains, and we both know this was no animal nor human – too many sound variations to it for either. We believe it was a demon or spirit.....

~ ~ ~

Let's end on a couple of very unnerving incidents;

'A couple of years ago, my buddy and I decide to go for a drive. It's summer and hot and we were bored, so we get in his car and decide to drive up the mountain about an hour away from us. It's another hour's drive to get to the top of it and the roads are pretty precarious with tight bends.'

'It's pretty late, around 3 a.m. by the time we get to the mountain and start driving up it but we don't have to be up for work the next day. It's totally quiet, no other cars there and we're both really chilled. The road twists until you get to the peak so you can barely see round each corner and its pitch dark apart from some road lights. As we go round one of the bends I start to get this really weird uneasy feeling as I see something really strange. There's a person sitting on a boulder right at the edge. My friend's seen them too but carries on driving, and I'm thinking wtf but then I see he's turning the car round carefully and slowly and going to go back.'

So we head back but I can tell he's still calm, not like me, so I tell myself it's just some crazy hiker. He stops the car dead beside the figure on the bolder and he shouts out to them, asking them if they're ok. I have to admit I'm pretty freaked so I keep quiet.

There's no response. Then the figure looks up and straight at us and we get the sh...t totally scared out of us. We see that it's a woman and she's wearing a long dress and she has beautiful long hair but it's her face; her face is like three times the length of a normal person's face and her eyes are completely empty; she's just staring at us blankly but she has this big creepy smile on her face.

I swear we both were so scared we couldn't move. We were completely frozen. We coudn't move, we coudln't say anything. I don't know how he managed to get his foot on the pedal and move the car and get us out of there, but i do know that when we got home, both of us were ill for quite a few days after that....'

~ ~ ~

'This happened when I was 16. My cousin and I were spending the weekend at our family cabin in the Mark Twain National Park. It was around 11 p.m. and we were in the back room playing a computer game and chatting. My cousin suddenly jumped up with a terrified squeal and pointed at the window. "Something was looking at us!"

'I would have said, yeah, funny, were it not for the fact that my cousin's face was white as a ghost. I asked him what was it? He said he saw it only for a fraction of a second and then it vanished but he said it wasn't human. My dog started barking at that moment. He was a Rottweiler. He wasn't scared of anything, but when we opened the door he was rooted to the spot, just staring at the front door with his teeth bared.'

'Now I was scared. We stood there for several minutes, too afraid to move and having no-where to go anyway. Nothing happened but I turned and went into the bedroom and grabbed our family's rifle. Slowly, very slowly, I opened the front door of the cabin and told my dog to chase them.'

'He would never have hesitated before, he would have done exactly that; but now, he wouldn't move. He was literally cowering at my feet. I couldn't see anything outside but I could not get the dog to move.

We heard something on the roof. It sounded like something ran from the back of the roof to the front, then we heard something drop down onto the front deck and heard it go under the deck but couldn't see it.'

'I shouted with as much conviction as I could, that I had a gun. Then I heard the most frightening sound I've ever heard in my entire life. Whatever was under the deck made this high-pitched scream. We fled inside and slammed the door. We could hear it moving under the floor. None of the windows in the cabin had any blinds on them or curtains which made us so freaked by this stage.'

'We put all the lights on in the cabin and sat down in a corner away from the window with my gun loaded and ready to shoot whatever this thing was if it decided to come into the cabin. We heard another scream that chilled our blood and what sure sounded like the door knob of the front door being turned, then this awful scratching sound on the door.

'We waited like that, for hours. My hands gripped

around the gun and barley able to breathe from the tension. We waited like that until the sun came up and even then we didn't move immediately.'

'Finally we went outside and looked around. The window pane had deep scratches in it as well as the front door, but there were no footprints or paw prints anywhere. We packed up our stuff faster than we've ever moved before and got out of there. When we finally got back home, I asked my cousin to tell me what he saw in the window. He said he didn't get a proper look at it for long but that what he did see was a face with no hair, black eyes, and whatever it was, it was grinning at him……..'

~ ~ ~

I hope you enjoyed this collection. If you have had a creepy, strange, or inexplicable experience, do feel free to contact me. I am actively continuing to research & collect the strangest of stories.

Steph Young Author (facebook)

Stephenyoungauthor@hotmail.com

STALKED IN THE WOODS

Printed in Great Britain
by Amazon